experiment
CENTRAL

So-Z volume 4

experiment
CENTRAL

understanding scientific principles through projects

John T. Tanacredi & John Loret, General Editors

AN IMPRINT OF THE GALE GROUP

DETROIT · NEW YORK · SAN FRANCISCO
LONDON · BOSTON · WOODBRIDGE, CT

experiment
CENTRAL Understanding Scientific Principles Through Projects

Researched, developed, and illustrated by **Book Builders Incorporated**

John T. Tanacredi, *General Editor*
John Loret, *General Editor*

U•X•L Staff

Allison McNeill, *U•X•L Senior Editor*
Elizabeth Shaw, *U•X•L Associate Editor*
Carol DeKane Nagel, *U•X•L Managing Editor*
Thomas L. Romig, *U•X•L Publisher*
Meggin Condino, *Senior Analyst, New Product Development*

Shalice Shah-Caldwell, *Permissions Associate (Pictures)*

Rita Wimberley, *Senior Buyer*
Evi Seoud, *Assistant Production Manager*
Dorothy Maki, *Manufacturing Manager*
Mary Beth Trimper, *Production Director*

Eric Johnson, Tracey Rowens, *Senior Art Directors*

Pamela A. Reed, *Imaging Coordinator*
Christine O'Bryan, *Graphic Specialist*
Randy Basset, *Image Database Supervisor*
Barbara Yarrow, *Graphic Services Manager*

Linda Mahoney, LM Design, *Typesetting*

Library of Congress Cataloging-in-Publication Data.

Loret, John.
  Experiment central: understanding scientific principles through projects / John Loret, John T. Tanacredi.
      p. cm.
  Includes bibliographical references and index.
  Contents: v. 1. A-Ec — v. 2. El-L — v. 3. M-Sc — v. 4. So-Z
  Summary: Demonstrates scientific concepts by means of experiments, including step-by-step instructions, lists of materials, troubleshooter's guide, and interpretation and explanation of results.
  ISBN 0-7876-2892-1 (set). — ISBN 0-7876-2893-X (v. 1) — ISBN 0-7876-2894-8 (v.2) — ISBN 0-7876-2895-6 (v.3) — ISBN 0-7876-2896-4 (v. 4)
  1. Science-Experiments-Juvenile literature. [1. Science-Experiments. 2. Experiments.] I. Tanacredi, John T. II. Title.
Q164 .L57 2000
507'.8-dc21   99-054142

contents

Volume 1: A-Ec

contents

Volume 2: El-L

Volume 3: M-Sc

experiment
CENTRAL

contents

Volume 4: So-Z

contents

reader's guide

Experiment Central: Understanding Scientific Principles Through Projects provides in one resource a wide variety of experiments covering nine key science curriculum fields—Astronomy, Biology, Botany, Chemistry, Ecology, Geology, Meteorology, Physics, and Scientific Method—spanning the earth sciences, life sciences, and physical sciences.

One hundred experiments and projects for students are presented in 50 subject-specific chapters. Chapters, each devoted to a scientific concept, include: Acid Rain, Biomes, Chemical Energy, Flight, Greenhouse Effect, Optics, Solar Energy, Stars, Volcanoes, and Weather. Two experiments or projects are provided in each chapter.

Entry format

Chapters are arranged alphabetically by scientific concept and are presented in a standard, easy-to-follow format. All chapters open with an explanatory overview section designed to introduce students to the scientific concept and provide the background behind a concept's discovery or important figures who helped advance the study of the field.

Each experiment is divided into eight standard sections designed to help students follow the experimental process clearly from beginning to end. Sections are:

- Purpose/Hypothesis
- Level of Difficulty
- Materials Needed
- Approximate Budget

- Timetable
- Step-by-Step Instructions
- Summary of Results
- Change the Variables

reader's guide

Each chapter also includes a "Design Your Own Experiment" section that allows students to apply what they have learned about a particular concept and create their own experiments. This section is divided into:

- How to Select a Topic Relating to this Concept
- Steps in the Scientific Method
- Recording Data and Summarizing the Results
- Related Projects

Concluding all chapters is a "For More Information" section that provides students with a list of books with further information about that particular topic.

Special Features

- A "Words to Know" section runs in the margin of each chapter providing definitions of terms used in that chapter. Terms in this list are bolded in the text upon first usage. A cumulative glossary collected from all "Words to Know" sections in the 50 chapters is included in the beginning of each volume.

- **Experiments by Scientific Field** index categorizes all 100 experiments by scientific curriculum area.

- **Parent's and Teacher's Guide** recommends that a responsible adult always oversee a student's experiment and provides several safety guidelines for all students to follow.

- Standard sidebar boxes accompany experiments and projects:

  "What Are the Variables?" explains the factors that may have an impact on the outcome of a particular experiment.

  "How to Experiment Safely" clearly explains any risks involved with the experiment and how to avoid them. While all experiments have been constructed with safety in mind, it is always recommended to proceed with caution and work under adult supervision while performing any experiment (please refer to Parent's and Teacher's Guide on page xvii).

  "Troubleshooter's Guide" presents problems that a student might encounter with an experiment, possible causes of the problem, and ways to remedy the problem.

- **Budget Index** categorizes experiments by approximate cost. Budgets may vary depending on what materials are readily available in the average household.

- **Level of Difficulty Index** lists experiments according to "Easy," "Moderate," "Difficult," or combination thereof. Level of difficulty is determined by such factors as the time necessary to complete the experiment, level of adult supervision recommended, and skill level of the average student. Level of difficulty will vary depending on the student. A teacher or parent should always be consulted before any experiment is attempted.

- **Timetable Index** categorizes each experiment by the time needed to complete it, including set-up and follow-through time. Times given are approximate.

- **General Subject Index** provides access to all major terms, people, places, and topics covered in *Experiment Central*.

- Approximately **150 photographs** enhance the text.

- Approximately **300 drawings** illustrate specific steps in the experiments, helping students follow the experimental procedure.

Acknowledgments

Credit is due to the general editors of *Experiment Central* who lent their time and expertise to the project, and oversaw compilation of the volumes and their contents:

John T. Tanacredi, Ph.D.
    Adjunct Full Professor of Ecology
    Department of Civil and Environmental Engineering,
    Polytechnic University
    Adjunct Full Professor of Environmental Sciences,
    Nassau Community College, State University of New York
    President, The Science Museum of Long Island

John Loret, Ph.D., D.Sc.
    Professor Emeritus and Former Director of Environmental
    Studies of Queens College, City University of New York
    Director, The Science Museum of Long Island

A note of appreciation is extended to the *Experiment Central* advisors, who provided their input when this work was in its formative stages:

reader's guide

Linda Barr
Editor and Writer for Book Builders Incorporated

Teresa F. Bettac
Middle School Advanced Science Teacher
Delaware, Ohio

Linda Leuzzi
Writer, Trustee of The Science Museum of Long Island

David J. Miller
Director of Education
The Science Museum of Long Island

Gracious thanks are also extended to science copyeditor Chris Cavette for his invaluable comments, expertise, and dedication to the project.

Comments and Suggestions

We welcome your comments on *Experiment Central*. Please write: Editors, *Experiment Central*, U•X•L, 27500 Drake Rd., Farmington Hills, Michigan, 48331–3535; call toll free: 1–800–877–4253; fax: 248–414–5043; or send e-mail via http://www.galegroup.com.

experiment
CENTRAL

parent's and teacher's guide

The experiments and projects in *Experiment Central* have been carefully constructed with issues of safety in mind, but your guidance and supervision are still required. Following the safety guidelines that accompany each experiment and project (found in the "How to Experiment Safely" sidebar box), as well as putting to work the safe practices listed below, will help your child or student avoid accidents. Oversee your child or student during experiments, and make sure he or she follows these safety guidelines:

- Always wear safety goggles if there is any possibility of sharp objects, small particles, splashes of liquid, or gas fumes getting in someone's eyes.

- Always wear protective gloves when handling materials that could irritate the skin.

- Never leave an open flame, such as a lit candle, unattended. Never wear loose clothing around an open flame.

- Follow instructions carefully when using electrical equipment, including batteries, to avoid getting shocked.

- Be cautious when handling sharp objects or glass equipment that might break. Point scissors away from you and use them carefully.

- Always ask for help in cleaning up spills, broken glass, or other hazardous materials.

- Always use protective gloves when handling hot objects. Set them down only on a protected surface that will not be damaged by heat.

- Always wash your hands thoroughly after handling material that might contain harmful microorganisms, such as soil and pond water.

- Do not substitute materials in an experiment without asking a knowledgeable adult about possible reactions.

- Do not use or mix unidentified liquids or powders. The result might be an explosion or poisonous fumes.

- Never taste or eat any substances being used in an experiment.

- Always wear old clothing or a protective apron to avoid staining your clothes.

experiments by scientific field

Chapter name in
brackets, followed
by experiment name;
bold type indicates
volume number, followed
by page number.

Botany

Chemistry

Ecology

experiments by scientific field

experiment
CENTRAL

Geology

Meteorology

Physics

All Subjects

**experiments
by scientific
field**

words to know

A

Abscission: The point at which a leaf meets a twig.

Acceleration: The rate at which the velocity and/or direction of an object is changing with the respect to time.

Acid: Substance that when dissolved in water is capable of reacting with a base to form salts and release hydrogen ions.

Acid rain: A form of precipitation that is significantly more acidic than neutral water, often produced as the result of industrial processes.

Acoustics: The science concerned with the production, properties, and propagation of sound waves.

Active solar energy system: A solar energy system that uses pumps or fans to circulate heat captured from the Sun.

Adhesion: Attraction between two different substances.

Aeration: Shaking a liquid to allow trapped gases to escape and to add oxygen.

Aerobic: Requiring oxygen.

Aerodynamics: The study of the motion of gases (particularly air) and the motion and control of objects in the air.

Alga/Algae: Single-celled or multicellular plants or plantlike organisms that contain chlorophyll, thus making their own food by photosynthesis. Algae grow mainly in water.

Alignment: Adjustment to a certain direction or orientation.

Alkaline: Having a pH of more than 7.

Alloy: A mixture of two or more metals with properties different from those metals of which it is made.

Amine: An organic compound derived from ammonia.

Amphibians: Animals that live on land and breathe air but return to the water to reproduce.

Amplitude: The maximum displacement (difference between an original position and a later position) of the material that is vibrating. Amplitude can be thought of visually as the highest and lowest points of a wave.

Anaerobic: Functioning without oxygen.

Anemometer: A device that measures wind speed.

Animalcules: Life forms that Anton van Leeuwenhoek named when he first saw them under his microscope; they later became known as protozoa and bacteria.

Anthocyanin: Red pigment found in leaves, petals, stems, and other parts of a plant.

Antibody: A protein produced by certain cells of the body as an immune (disease-fighting) response to a specific foreign antigen.

Aquifer: Underground layer of sand, gravel, or spongy rock that collects water.

Arch: A curved structure spanning an opening that supports a wall or other weight above the opening.

Artesian well: A well in which water is under pressure.

Asexual reproduction: Any reproductive process that does not involve the union of two individuals in the exchange of genetic material.

Astronomers: Scientists who study the positions, motions, and composition of stars and other objects in the sky.

Astronomy: The study of the physical properties of objects and matter outside Earth's atmosphere.

Atmosphere: Layers of air that surround Earth.

Atmospheric pressure: The pressure exerted by the atmosphere at Earth's surface due to the weight of the air.

Atom: The smallest unit of an element, made up of protons and neutrons in a central nucleus surrounded by moving electrons.

Autotroph: An organism that can build all the food and produce all the energy it needs with its own resources.

Auxins: A group of plant hormones responsible for patterns of plant growth.

B

Bacteria: Single-celled microorganisms that live in soil, water, plants, and animals that play a key role in the decaying of organic matter and the cycling of nutrients. Some are agents of disease.

Bacteriology: The scientific study of bacteria, their characteristics, and their activities as related to medicine, industry, and agriculture.

Base: Substance that when dissolved in water is capable of reacting with an acid to form salts and release hydrogen ions; has a pH of more than 7.

Beriberi: A disease caused by a deficiency of thiamine and characterized by nerve and gastrointestinal disorders.

Biochemical oxygen demand (BOD_5): The amount of oxygen that microorganisms use over a five-day period in 68° Fahrenheit (20° Celsius) water to decay organic matter.

Biological variables: Living factors such as bacteria, fungi, and animals that can affect the processes that occur in nature and in an experiment.

Biomes: Large geographical areas with specific climates and soils, as well as distinct plant and animal communities that are interdependent.

Bond: The force that holds two atoms together.

Botany: The branch of biology involving the study of plant life.

Braided rivers: Wide, shallow rivers with pebbly islands in the middle.

Buoyancy: The tendency of a fluid to exert a lifting effect on a body immersed in it.

By-products: Something produced in the making of something else.

c

Calibration: Standardizing or adjusting a measuring instrument so its measurements are correct.

Capillary action: The tendency of water to rise through a narrow tube by the force of adhesion between the water and the walls of the tube.

Carbohydrate: A compound consisting of carbon, hydrogen, and oxygen found in plants and used as a food by humans and other animals.

Carnivore: Meat-eating organism.

Carotene: Yellowish-orange pigment present in most leaves.

Catalyst: A compound that speeds up the rate of a chemical reaction without undergoing any change in its own composition.

Celestial: Describing planets or other objects in space.

Cell: The basic unit of a living organism; cells are structured to perform highly specialized functions.

Cell membrane: The thin layer of tissue that surrounds a cell.

Cell theory: The idea that all living things have one or more similar cells that carry out the same functions for the living process.

Centrifuge: A device that rapidly spins a solution so that the heavier components will separate from the lighter ones.

Centripetal force: Rotating force that moves towards the center or axis.

Channel: A shallow trench carved into the ground by the pressure and movement of a river.

Chemical energy: Energy stored in chemical bonds.

Chemical property: A characteristic of a substance that allows it to undergo a chemical change. Chemical properties include flammability and sensitivity to light.

Chemical reaction: Any chemical change in which at least one new substance is formed.

Chlorophyll: A green pigment found in plants that absorbs sunlight, providing the energy used in photosynthesis, or the conversion of carbon dioxide and water to complex carbohydrates.

experiment
CENTRAL

Chloroplasts: Small structures in plant cells that contain chlorophyll and in which the process of photosynthesis takes place.

Chromatography: A method for separating mixtures into their component parts (into their "ingredients," or into what makes them up).

Circuit: The complete path of an electric current including the source of electric energy.

Cleavage: The tendency of a mineral to split along certain planes.

Climate: The average weather that a region experiences over a long period.

Coagulation: The clumping together of particles in a liquid.

Cohesion: Attraction between like substances.

Colloid: A mixture containing particles suspended in, but not dissolved in, a dispersing medium.

Colony: A mass of microorganisms that have been bred in a medium.

Combustion: Any chemical reaction in which heat, and usually light, is produced. It is commonly the burning of organic substances during which oxygen from the air is used to form carbon dioxide and water vapor.

Complete metamorphosis: Metamorphosis in which a larva becomes a pupa before changing into an adult form.

Composting: The process in which organic compounds break down and become dark, fertile soil called humus.

Concave: Hollowed or rounded upward, like the inside of a bowl; arched.

Concentration: The amount of a substance present in a given volume, such as the number of molecules in a liter.

Condense/condensation: The process by which a gas changes into a liquid.

Conduction: The flow of heat through a solid.

Confined aquifer: An aquifer with a layer of impermeable rock above it; the water is held under pressure.

Coniferous: Refers to trees, such as pines and firs, that bear cones and have needle-like leaves that are not shed all at once.

Constellations: Eighty-eight patterns of stars in the night sky.

Continental drift: The theory that continents move apart slowly at a predictable rate.

Control experiment: A set-up that is identical to the experiment but is not affected by the variable that will be changed during the experiment.

Convection: The circulatory motion that occurs in a gas or liquid at a nonuniform temperature; the variation of the motion is caused by the substance's density and the action of gravity.

Convection current: Circular movement of a fluid in response to alternating heating and cooling.

Convex: Curved or rounded like the outside of a ball.

Corona: The outermost atmospheric layer of the Sun.

Corrosion: An oxidation-reduction reaction in which a metal is oxidized (reacted with oxygen) and oxygen is reduced, usually in the presence of moisture.

Cotyledon: Seed leaves, which contain stored food for the embryo.

Crust: The hard, outer shell of Earth that floats upon the softer, denser mantle.

Cultures: Microorganisms growing in prepared nutrients.

Cyanobacteria: Oxygen-producing, aquatic bacteria capable of manufacturing its own food; resembles algae.

Cycle: Occurrence of events that take place the same time every year; a single complete vibration.

Cytology: The branch of biology concerned with the study of cells.

Cytoplasm: The semifluid substance inside a cell that surrounds the nucleus and the other membrane-enclosed organelles.

D

Decanting: The process of separating a suspension by waiting for its heavier components to settle out and then pouring off the lighter ones.

Decibel (dB): A unit of measurement for sound.

Deciduous: Plants that lose their leaves at some season of the year, and then grow them back at another season.

Decomposition: The breakdown of complex molecules—molecules of which dead organisms are composed—into simple nutrients that can be reutilized by living organisms.

Decomposition reaction: A chemical reaction in which one substance is broken down into two or more substances.

Denaturization: Altering of an enzyme so it no longer works.

Density: The mass of a substance compared to its volume.

Density ball: A ball with the fixed standard of 1.0 g/l, which is the exact density of pure water.

Dependent variable: The variable in a function whose value depends on the value of another variable in the function.

Deposition: Dropping of sediments that occurs when a river loses its energy of motion.

Desert: A biome with a hot-to-cool climate and dry weather.

Desertification: Transformation of arid or semiarid productive land into desert.

Dewpoint: The point at which water vapor begins to condense.

Dicot: Plants with a pair of embryonic seeds that appear at germination.

Diffraction: The bending of light or another form of electromagnetic radiation as it passes through a tiny hole or around a sharp edge.

Diffraction grating: A device consisting of a surface into which are etched very fine, closely spaced grooves that cause different wavelengths of light to reflect or refract (bend) by different amounts.

Diffusion: Random movement of molecules that leads to a net movement of molecules from a region of high concentration to a region of low concentration.

Disinfection: Using chemicals to kill harmful organisms.

Dissolved oxygen (DO): Oxygen molecules that have dissolved in water.

Distillation: The process of separating liquids from solids or from other liquids with different boiling points by a method of evaporation and condensation, so that each component in a mixture can be collected separately in its pure form.

DNA: Abbreviation for deoxyribonucleic acid. Large, complex molecules found in nuclei of cells that carry genetic information for an organism's development.

Domain: Small regions in an iron object that possess their own magnetic charges.

Dormancy: A state of inactivity in an organism.

Dormant: Describing an inactive organism.

Drought: A prolonged period of dry weather that damages crops or prevents their growth.

Dry cell: An electrolytic cell or battery using a non-liquid electrolyte.

Dynamic equilibrium: A situation in which substances are moving into and out of cell walls at an equal rate.

E

Earthquake: An unpredictable event in which masses of rock shift below Earth's surface, releasing enormous amounts of energy and sending out shock waves that sometimes cause the ground to shake dramatically.

Eclipse: A phenomenon in which the light from a celestial body is temporarily cut off by the presence of another body.

Ecologists: Scientists who study the interrelationship of organisms and their environments.

Ecosystem: An ecological community, including plants, animals and microorganisms considered together with their environment.

Electric charge repulsion: Repulsion of particles caused by a layer of negative ions surrounding each particle. The repulsion prevents coagulation and promotes the even dispersion of such particles through a mixture.

Electrical energy: The motion of electrons within any object that conducts electricity.

experiment
CENTRAL

Electricity: A form of energy caused by the presence of electrical charges in matter.

Electrode: A material that will conduct an electrical current, usually a metal; used to carry electrons into or out of an electrochemical cell.

Electrolyte: Any substance that, when dissolved in water, conducts an electric current.

Electromagnetic spectrum: The complete array of electromagnetic radiation, including radio waves (at the longest-wavelength end), microwaves, infrared radiation, visible light, ultraviolet radiation, X rays, and gamma rays (at the shortest-wavelength end).

Electromagnetic waves: Radiation that has properties of both an electric and a magnetic wave and that travels through a vacuum at the speed of light.

Electromagnetism: A form of magnetic energy produced by the flow of an electric current through a metal core. Also, the study of electric and magnetic fields and their interaction with charges and currents.

Electron: A subatomic particle with a mass of about one atomic mass unit and a single electrical charge that orbits the nucleus of an atom.

Electroscope: A device that determines whether an object is electrically charged.

Elevation: Height above sea level.

Elliptical: An orbital path that is egg-shaped or resembles an elongated circle.

Embryo: The seed of a plant, which through germination can develop into a new plant; also, the earliest stage of animal development.

Embryonic: The earliest stages of development.

Endothermic reaction: A chemical reaction that absorbs energy, such as photosynthesis, the production of food by plant cells.

Energy: The ability to cause an action or for work to be done. Also, power that can be used to perform work, such as solar energy.

Environmental variables: Nonliving factors such as air temperature, water, pollution, and pH that can affect processes that occur in nature and in an experiment.

Enzymes: Any of numerous complex proteins produced by living cells that act as catalysts, speeding up the rate of chemical reactions in living organisms.

Enzymology: The science of studying enzymes.

Ephemerals: Plants that lie dormant in dry soil for years until major rainstorms occur.

Epicenter: The location where the seismic waves of an earthquake first appear on the surface, usually almost directly above the focus.

Equilibrium: A process in which the rates at which various changes take place balance each other, resulting in no overall change.

Erosion: The process by which topsoil is carried away by water, wind, or ice.

Eutrophic zone: The upper part of the ocean where sunlight penetrates, supporting plant life such as phytoplankton.

Eutrophication: Natural process by which a lake or other body of water becomes enriched in dissolved nutrients, spurring aquatic plant growth.

Evaporate/evaporation: The process by which liquid changes into a gas; also, the escape of water vapor into the air, yielding only the solute.

Exothermic reaction: A chemical reaction that releases energy, such as the burning of fuel.

Experiment: A controlled observation.

F

Fat: A type of lipid, or chemical compound used as a source of energy, to provide insulation, and to protect organs in an animal's body.

Fault: A crack running through rock that is the result of tectonic forces.

Fault blocks: Pieces of rock from Earth's crust that overlap and cause earthquakes when they press together and snap from pressure.

Filtration: The use of a screen or filter to separate larger particles from smaller ones that can slip through the filter's openings.

Fluorescence: Luminescence (glowing) that stops within 10 nanoseconds after an energy source has been removed.

Focal length: The distance of a focus from the surface of a lens or concave mirror.

Focal point: The point at which rays of light converge (come together) or from which they diverge (move apart).

Food web: An interconnected set of all the food chains in the same ecosystem.

Force: A physical interaction (pushing or pulling) tending to change the state of motion (velocity) of an object.

Fossil fuel: A fuel such as coal, oil, or natural gas that is formed over millions of years from the remains of plants and animals.

Fracture: A mineral's tendency to break into curved, rough, or jagged surfaces.

Frequency: The rate at which vibrations take place (number of times per second the motion is repeated), given in cycles per second or in hertz (Hz). Also, the number of waves that pass a given point in a given period of time.

Front: The front edges of moving masses of air.

Fungus: Kingdom of various single-celled or multicellular organisms, including mushrooms, molds, yeasts, and mildews, that do not contain chlorophyll. (Plural is fungi.)

Fusion: Combining of nuclei of two or more lighter elements into one nucleus of a heavier element; the process stars use to produce energy to support themselves against their own gravity.

G

Galaxy: A large collection of stars and clusters of stars containing anywhere from a few million to a few trillion stars.

Gene: A segment of a DNA (deoxyribonucleic acid) molecule contained in the nucleus of a cell that acts as a kind of code for the production of some specific protein. Genes carry instructions for the formation, functioning, and transmission of specific traits from one generation to another.

Genetic material: Material that transfers characteristics from a parent to its offspring.

Geology: The study of the origin, history, and structure of Earth.

Geotropism: The tendency of roots to bend toward Earth.

Germ theory of disease: The belief that disease is caused by germs.

Germination: The beginning of growth of a seed.

Gibbous moon: A phase of the Moon when more than half of its surface is lighted.

Glacier: A large mass of ice formed from snow that has packed together and which moves slowly down a slope under its own weight.

Global warming: Warming of Earth's atmosphere that results from an increase in the concentration of gases that store heat such as carbon dioxide.

Glucose: Also known as blood sugar; a simple sugar broken down in cells to produce energy.

Golgi body: Organelle that sorts, modifies, and packages molecules.

Gravity: Force of attraction between objects, the strength of which depends on the mass of each object and the distance between them.

Greenhouse effect: The warming of Earth's atmosphere due to water vapor, carbon dioxide, and other gases in the atmosphere that trap heat radiated from Earth's surface.

Greenhouse gases: Gases that absorb infrared radiation and warm air before it escapes into space.

Groundwater: Water that soaks into the ground and is stored in the small spaces between the rocks and soil.

H

Heat: A form of energy produced by the motion of molecules that make up a substance.

Heat energy: The energy produced when two substances that have different temperatures are combined.

Herbivore: Plant-eating organism.

experiment
CENTRAL

Hertz (Hz): The unit of frequency; a measure of the number of waves that pass a given point per second of time.

Heterotrophs: Organisms that cannot make their own food and that must, therefore, obtain their food from other organisms.

High air pressure: An area where the air molecules are more dense.

Hormone: A chemical produced in living cells that regulates the functions of the organism.

Humidity: The amount of water vapor (moisture) contained in the air.

Humus: Fragrant, spongy, nutrient-rich decayed plant or animal matter.

Hydrologic cycle: Continual movement of water from the atmosphere to Earth's surface through precipitation and back to the atmosphere through evaporation and transpiration.

Hydrologists: Scientists who study water and its cycle.

Hydrology: The study of water and its cycle.

Hydrometer: An instrument that determines the specific gravity of a liquid.

Hydrophilic: A substance that is attracted to and readily mixes with water.

Hydrophobic: A substance that is repelled by and does not mix with water.

Hydrotropism: The tendency of roots to grow toward a water source.

Hypertonic solution: A solution with a higher osmotic pressure (solute concentration) than another solution.

Hypothesis: An idea in the form of a statement that can be tested by observation and/or experiment.

Hypotonic solution: A solution with a lower osmotic pressure (solute concentration) than another solution.

I

Igneous rock: Rock formed from the cooling and hardening of magma.

Immiscible: Incapable of being mixed.

Impermeable: Not allowing substances to pass through.

Impurities: Chemicals or other pollutants in water.

Incomplete metamorphosis: Metamorphosis in which a nymph form gradually becomes an adult through molting.

Independent variable: The variable in a function that determines the final value of the function.

Indicator: Pigments that change color when they come into contact with acidic or basic solutions.

Inertia: The tendency of an object to continue in its state of motion.

Infrared radiation: Electromagnetic radiation of a wavelength shorter than radio waves but longer than visible light that takes the form of heat.

Inner core: Very dense, solid center of Earth.

Inorganic: Not made of or coming from living things.

Insulated wire: Electrical wire coated with a nonconducting material such as plastic.

Insulation/insulator: A material that does not conduct heat or electricity.

Interference fringes: Bands of color that fan around an object.

Ion: An atom or group of atoms that carries an electrical charge— either positive or negative—as a result of losing or gaining one or more electrons.

Ionic conduction: The flow of an electrical current by the movement of charged particles, or ions.

Isobars: Continuous lines on a map that connect areas with the same air pressure.

Isotonic solutions: Two solutions that have the same concentration of solute particles and therefore the same osmotic pressure.

K

Kinetic energy: Energy of an object or system due to its motion.

L

Lactobacilli: A strain of bacteria.

Larva: Immature form (wormlike in insects; fishlike in amphibians) of an organism capable of surviving on its own. A larva does not resemble the parent and must go through metamorphosis, or change, to reach its adult stage.

Lava: Molten rock that occurs at the surface of Earth, usually through volcanic eruptions.

Lens: A piece of transparent material with two curved surfaces that bring together and focus rays of light passing through it.

Lichen: An organism composed of a fungus and a photosynthetic organism in a symbiotic relationship.

Lift: Upper force on the wings of an aircraft created by differences in air pressure on top of and underneath the wings.

Light-year: Distance light travels in one year in the vacuum of space, roughly 5.9 trillion miles (9.5 trillion km).

The Local Group: A cluster of 30 galaxies, including the Milky Way, pulled together gravitationally.

Low air pressure: An area where the air molecules are less dense.

Lunar eclipse: Eclipse that occurs when Earth passes between the Sun and the Moon, casting a shadow on the Moon.

Luster: A glow of reflected light; a sheen.

M

Macroorganisms: Visible organisms that aid in breaking down organic matter.

Magma: Molten rock deep within Earth that consists of liquids, gases, and particles of rocks and crystals. Magma underlies areas of volcanic activity and at Earth's surface is called lava.

Magma chambers: Pools of bubbling liquid rock that are the energy sources causing volcanoes to be active.

Magma surge: A swell or rising wave of magma caused by the movement and friction of tectonic plates; the surge heats and melts rock, adding to the magma and its force.

Magnet: A material that attracts other like material, especially metals.

Magnetic circuit: A series of magnetic domains aligned in the same direction.

Magnetic field: The space around an electric current or a magnet in which a magnetic force can be observed.

Magnetism: A fundamental force of nature caused by the motion of electrons in an atom. Magnetism is manifested by the attraction of certain materials for iron.

Mantle: Thick, dense layer of rock that underlies Earth's crust and overlies the core.

Manure: The waste matter of animals.

Mass: Measure of the total amount of matter in an object. Also, an object's quantity of matter as shown by its gravitational pull on another object.

Matter: Anything that has mass and takes up space.

Meandering river: A lowland river that twists and turns along its route to the sea.

Medium: A material that carries the acoustic vibrations away from the body producing them.

Meniscus: The curved surface of a column of liquid.

Metamorphic rock: Rock formed by transformation of pre-existing rock through changes in temperature and pressure.

Metamorphosis: Transformation of an immature animal into an adult.

Meteorologists: Scientists who study weather and weather forecasting.

Microbiology: Branch of biology dealing with microscopic forms of life.

Microclimate: A local climate.

Microorganisms: Living organisms so small that they can be seen only with the aid of a microscope.

Micropyle: Seed opening that enables water to enter easily.

Milky Way: The galaxy in which our solar system is located.

Mineral: An inorganic substance found in nature with a definite chemical composition and structure. As a nutrient, helps build bones and soft tissues and regulates body functions.

Mixtures: Combinations of two or more substances that are not chemically combined with each other and can exist in any proportion.

Molecule: The smallest particle of a substance that retains all the properties of the substance and is composed of one or more atoms.

Molting: Shedding of the outer layer of an animal, as occurs during growth of insect larvae.

Monocot: Plants with a single embryonic seed at germination.

Moraine: Mass of boulders, stones, and other rock debris carried along and deposited by a glacier.

Multicellular: Living things with many cells joined together.

N

Nanometer: A unit of length; this measurement is equal to one-billionth of a meter.

Nansen bottles: Self-closing containers with thermometers that draw in water at different depths.

Nebula: Bright or dark cloud, often composed of gases and dust, hovering in the space between the stars.

Neutralization: A chemical process in which the mixing of an acidic solution with a basic (alkaline) solution results in a solution that has the properties of neither an acid nor a base.

Neutron: A subatomic particle with a mass of about one atomic mass unit and no electrical charge that is found in the nucleus of an atom.

Niche: The specific role that an organism carries out in its ecosystem.

Nonpoint source: An unidentified source of pollution; may actually be a number of sources.

Nucleus: The central core of an atom, consisting of protons and (usually) neutrons.

Nutrient: A substance needed by an organism in order for it to survive, grow, and develop.

Nutrition: The study of the food nutrients an organism needs in order to maintain well-being.

Nymph: An immature form in the life cycle of insects that go through an incomplete metamorphosis.

O

Oceanography: The study of the chemistry of the oceans, as well as their currents, marine life, and the ocean bed.

Optics: The study of the nature of light and its properties.

Organelles: Membrane-bounded cellular "organs" performing a specific set of functions within a eukaryotic cell.

Organic: Made of or coming from living things.

Osmosis: The movement of fluids and substances dissolved in liquids across a semipermeable membrane from an area of its greater concentration to an area of its lesser concentration until all substances involved reach a balance.

Outer core: A liquid core that surrounds Earth's solid inner core; made mostly of iron.

Oxidation: A chemical reaction in which oxygen reacts with some other substance and in which ions, atoms, or molecules lose electrons.

Oxidation-reduction reaction: A chemical reaction in which one substance loses one or more electrons and the other substance gains one or more electrons.

Oxidation state: The sum of an atom's positive and negative charges.

Oxidizing agent: A chemical substance that gives up oxygen or takes on electrons from another substance.

Ozone layer: The atmospheric layer of approximately 15 to 30 miles (24 to 48 km) above Earth's surface in which the concentration of ozone is significantly higher than in other parts of the atmosphere and that protects the lower atmosphere from harmful solar radiation.

P

Papain: An enzyme obtained from the fruit of the papaya used as a meat tenderizer, as a drug to clean cuts and wounds, and as a digestive aid for stomach disorders.

Passive solar energy system: A solar energy system in which the heat of the Sun is captured, used, and stored by means of the design of a building and the materials from which it is made.

Pasteurization: The process of slow heating that kills bacteria and other microorganisms.

Penicillin: A mold from the fungi group of microorganisms used as an antibiotic.

Pepsin: Digestive enzyme that breaks down protein.

Percolate: To pass through a permeable substance.

Permeable: Having pores that permit a liquid or a gas to pass through.

pH: Abbreviation for potential hydrogen. A measure of the acidity or alkalinity of a solution determined by the concentration of hydrogen ions present in a liter of a given fluid. The pH scale ranges from 0 (greatest concentration of hydrogen ions and therefore most acidic) to 14 (least concentration of hydrogen ions and therefore most alkaline), with 7 representing a neutral solution, such as pure water.

Pharmacology: The science dealing with the properties, reactions, and therapeutic values of drugs.

Phases: Changes in the illuminated Moon surfaces as the Moon revolves around Earth.

Phloem: Plant tissue consisting of elongated cells that transport carbohydrates and other nutrients.

Phosphorescence: Luminescence (glowing) that stops within 10 nanoseconds after an energy source has been removed.

Photoelectric effect: The phenomenon in which light falling upon certain metals stimulates the emission of electrons and changes light into electricity.

Photosynthesis: Chemical process by which plants containing chlorophyll use sunlight to manufacture their own food by converting carbon dioxide and water to carbohydrates, releasing oxygen as a by-product.

Phototropism: The tendency of a plant to grow toward a source of light.

Photovoltaic cells: A device made of silicon that converts sunlight into electricity.

Physical change: A change in which the substance keeps its identity, such as a piece of chalk that has been ground up.

Physical property: A characteristic that you can detect with your senses, such as color and shape.

Phytoplankton: Microscopic aquatic plants that live suspended in the water.

Pigment: A substance that displays a color because of the wavelengths of light that it reflects.

Pitch: A property of a sound, determined by its frequency; the highness or lowness of a sound.

Plates: Large regions of Earth's surface, composed of the crust and uppermost mantle, which move about, forming many of Earth's major geologic surface features.

Pnematocysts: Stinging cells.

Point source: An identified source of pollution.

Pollination: The transfer of pollen from the male reproductive organs to the female reproductive organs of plants.

Pore: An opening or space.

Potential energy: The energy possessed by a body as a result of its position.

Precipitation: Water in its liquid or frozen form when it falls from clouds as rain, snow, sleet, or hail.

Probe: The terminal of a voltmeter, used to connect the voltmeter to a circuit.

Producer: An organism that can manufacture its own food from nonliving materials and an external energy source, usually by photosynthesis.

Product: A compound that is formed as a result of a chemical reaction.

Prominences: Masses of glowing gas, mainly hydrogen, that rise from the Sun's surface like flames.

Propeller: Radiating blades mounted on a quickly rotating shaft that are used to move aircraft forward.

Protein: A complex chemical compound that consists of many amino acids attached to each other that are essential to the structure and functioning of all living cells.

Protists: Members of the kingdom Protista, primarily single-celled organisms that are not plants or animals.

Proton: A subatomic particle with a mass of about one atomic mass unit and a single negative electrical change that is found in the nucleus of an atom.

Protozoan: Single-celled animal-like microscopic organisms that live by taking in food rather than making it by photosynthesis and must live in the presence of water. (Plural is protozoa.)

Pupa: A stage in the metamorphosis of an insect during which its tissues are completely reorganized to take on their adult shape.

R

Radiation: Energy transmitted in the form of electromagnetic waves or subatomic particles.

Radicule: A seed's root system.

Radio wave: Longest form of electromagnetic radiation, measuring up to 6 miles (9.6 km) from peak to peak.

Radiosonde balloons: Instruments for collecting data in the atmosphere and then transmitting that data back to Earth by means of radio waves.

Reactant: A compound present at the beginning of a chemical reaction.

Reaction: Response to an action prompted by a stimulus.

Reduction: A process in which a chemical substance gives off oxygen or takes on electrons.

Reflection: The bouncing of light rays in a regular pattern off the surface of an object.

Refraction: The bending of light rays as they pass at an angle from one transparent or clear medium into a second one of different density.

Rennin: Enzyme used in making cheese.

Resistance: A partial or complete limiting of the flow of electrical current through a material.

Respiration: The physical process that supplies oxygen to living cells and the chemical reactions that take place inside the cells.

Resultant: A force that results from the combined action of two other forces.

Retina: The light-sensitive part of the eyeball that receives images and transmits visual impulses through the optic nerve to the brain.

River: A main course of water into which many other smaller bodies of water flow.

Rock: Naturally occurring solid mixture of minerals.

Runoff: Water in excess of what can be absorbed by the ground.

s

Salinity: The amount of salts dissolved in seawater.

Saturated: Containing the maximum amount of a solute for a given amount of solvent at a certain temperature.

Scientific method: Collecting evidence meticulously and then theorizing from it.

Scribes: Ancient scholars.

Scurvy: A disease caused by a deficiency of vitamin C, which causes a weakening of connective tissue in bone and muscle.

Sediment: Sand, silt, clay, rock, gravel, mud, or other matter that has been transported by flowing water.

Sedimentary rock: Rock formed from the compressed and solidified layers of organic or inorganic matter.

Sedimentation: A process during which gravity pulls particles out of a liquid.

Seismic belt: Boundaries where Earth's plates meet.

Seismic waves: Classified as body waves or surface waves, vibrations in rock and soil that transfer the force of the earthquake from the focus (center) into the surrounding area.

Seismograph: A device that records vibrations of the ground and within Earth.

Seismology: The study and measurement of earthquakes.

Seismometer: A seismograph that measures the movement of the ground.

Semipermeable membrane: A thin barrier between two solutions that permits only certain components of the solutions, usually the solvent, to pass through.

Sexual reproduction: A reproductive process that involves the union of two individuals in the exchange of genetic material.

Silt: Medium-sized soil particles.

Solar collector: A device that absorbs sunlight and collects solar heat.

Solar eclipse: Eclipse that occurs when the Moon passes between Earth and the Sun, casting a shadow on Earth.

Solar energy: Any form of electromagnetic radiation that is emitted by the Sun.

Solute: The substance that is dissolved to make a solution and exists in the least amount in a solution, for example sugar in sugar water.

Solution: A mixture of two or more substances that appears to be uniform throughout except on a molecular level.

Solvent: The major component of a solution or the liquid in which some other component is dissolved, for example water in sugar water.

Specific gravity: The ratio of the density of a substance to the density of another substance.

Spectrum: Range of individual wavelengths of radiation produced when white light is broken down into its component colors when it passes through a prism or is broken apart by some other means.

Standard: A base for comparison.

Star: A vast clump of hydrogen gas and dust that produces great energy through fusion reactions at its core.

Static electricity: A form of electricity produced by friction in which the electric charge does not flow in a current but stays in one place.

Streak: The color of the dust left when a mineral is rubbed across a surface.

Substrate: The substance on which an enzyme operates in a chemical reaction.

Succulent: Plants that live in dry environments and have water storage tissue.

Surface water: Water in lakes, rivers, ponds, and streams.

Suspension: A temporary mixture of a solid in a gas or liquid from which the solid will eventually settle out.

Symbiosis: A pattern in which two or more organisms live in close connection with each other, often to the benefit of both or all organisms.

Synthesis reaction: A chemical reaction in which two or more substances combine to form a new substance.

T

Taiga: A large land biome mostly dominated by coniferous trees.

Tectonic plates: Huge flat rocks that form Earth's crust.

Temperate: Mild or moderate weather conditions.

Temperature: The measure of the average energy of the molecules in a substance.

Terminal: A connection in an electric circuit; usually a connection on a source of electric energy such as a battery.

Terracing: A series of horizontal ridges made in a hillside to reduce erosion.

Testa: A tough outer layer that protects the embryo and endosperm of a seed from damage.

Thermal conductivity: A number representing a material's ability to conduct heat.

Thermal energy: Energy caused by the movement of molecules due to the transfer of heat.

Thiamine: A vitamin of the B complex that is essential to normal metabolism and nerve function.

Thigmotropism: The tendency for a plant to grow toward a surface it touches.

Titration: A procedure in which an acid and a base are slowly mixed to achieve a neutral substance.

Toxic: Poisonous.

Trace element: A chemical element present in minute quantities.

Translucent: Permits the passage of light.

Tropism: The growth or movement of a plant toward or away from a stimulus.

Troposphere: The lowest layer of Earth's atmosphere, ranging to an altitude of about 9 miles (15 km) above Earth's surface.

Tsunami: A tidal wave caused by an earthquake.

Tuber: An underground, starch-storing stem, such as a potato.

Tundra: A treeless, frozen biome with low-lying plants.

Turbulence: Air disturbance or unrest that affects an aircraft's flight.

Tyndall effect: The effect achieved when colloidal particles reflect a beam of light, making it visible when shined through such a mixture.

U

Ultraviolet: Electromagnetic radiation (energy) of a wavelength just shorter than the violet (shortest wavelength) end of the visible light spectrum and thus with higher energy than the visible light.

Unconfined aquifer: An aquifer under a layer of permeable rock and soil.

Unicellular: Living things that have one cell. Protozoans are unicellular.

Universal gravitation: The notion of the constancy of the force of gravity between two bodies.

V

Vacuole: A space-filling organelle of plant cells.

Variable: Something that can change the results of an experiment.

Vegetative propagation: A form of asexual reproduction in which plants are produced that are genetically identical to the parent.

Viable: The capability of developing or growing under favorable conditions.

Vibration: A regular, back-and-forth motion of molecules in the air.

Visible spectrum: Light waves visible to the eye.

Vitamin: A complex organic compound found naturally in plants and animals that the body needs in small amounts for normal growth and activity.

Volcano: A conical mountain or dome of lava, ash, and cinders that forms around a vent leading to molten rock deep within Earth.

Voltage: Also called potential difference; the amount of electric energy stored in a mass of electric charges compared to the energy stored in some other mass of charges.

Voltmeter: An instrument for measuring the conductivity or resistance in a circuit or the voltage produced by an electric source.

Volume: The amount of space occupied by a three-dimensional object; the amplitude or loudness of a sound.

W

Water (hydrologic) cycle: The constant movement of water molecules on Earth as they rise into the atmosphere as water vapor, condense into droplets and fall to land or bodies of water, evaporate, and rise again.

Waterline: The highest point to which water rises on the hull of a ship. The portion of the hull below the waterline is under water.

Water table: The upper surface of groundwater.

Water vapor: Water in its gaseous state.

Wave: A motion in which energy and momentum is carried away from some source.

Wavelength: The distance between the peak of a wave of light, heat, or energy and the next corresponding peak.

Weather: The state of the troposphere at a particular time and place.

Weather forecasting: The scientific predictions of future weather patterns.

Weight: The gravitational attraction of Earth on an object; the measure of the heaviness of an object.

Wetlands: Areas that are wet or covered with water for at least part of the year.

X

Xanthophyll: Yellow pigment in plants.

Xerophytes: Plants that require little water to survive.

Xylem: Plant tissue consisting of elongated, thick-walled cells that transport water and mineral nutrients.

experiment
CENTRAL

chapter 38

Solar Energy

Sunlight has been recognized as a powerful source of energy since ancient times. "Burning glasses" that dated back to 7 B.C. have been found in the ruins of Nineva (now part of Iraq). These glasses were similar to magnifying lens and could concentrate sunlight into a beam hot enough to start a fire. Each day, Earth receives about 4 quadrillion kilowatt-hours of **solar energy**, generated by nuclear reactions deep inside the Sun's mass. While we receive a lot of solar energy, it is not easy to harness. Environmental concerns and our limited supply of fossil fuels make finding ways to gather and concentrate solar energy efficiently an urgent challenge.

Hot! Hot! Hot!

Think of the Sun as a constantly active hydrogen bomb: a swirling, mass with eruptions that give off great amounts of energy. Within the Sun's center, the temperature is about 25,000,000°F (14,000,000°C). About 700 million tons (635 million metric tons) of hydrogen fuse into 695 million tons (630 million metric tons) of helium each second. What happens to the missing five million tons of material? It is converted into solar energy. Besides heating and illuminating the Sun itself, some of this energy travels to Earth as sunlight.

How is some of this energy collected? One way is through the use of **solar collectors**, flat devices made of aluminum, copper, or steel panels painted black. The black color helps to absorb the heat energy. The glass or plastic covering these panels enables light to enter, but prevents most of the heat from bouncing back into the atmosphere.

Words to Know

Active solar energy system:
A solar energy system that uses pumps or fans to circulate heat captured from the Sun.

Efficiency:
The amount of power output divided by the amount of power input. It is a measure of how well a device converts one form of power into another.

Solar eruptions like this one could provide us with enough power for thousands of years—if we could harness the energy.

The heat is then stored in a layer of pebbles or salt surrounded by a thick layer of insulation behind the black panel.

This type of solar energy collection is an **active solar energy system.** An active system requires a separate collector, as well as a storage device and pumps or fans that draw heat when needed. **Passive solar energy systems** use the design of the building or natural materials to collect the Sun's energy. One example is buildings with large windows that face south, allowing the Sun's heat to spread throughout the structure during the day. This process is similar to the **greenhouse effect**, in which the Sun's energy gets trapped near Earth's surface by gases and other atmospheric matter.

Various forms of passive solar energy systems have been applied for centuries. For example, buildings were constructed with thick walls of stone, sod, and adobe to absorb the Sun's heat during the day and release it at night. Greenhouses were used in the early 1800s to capture the Sun's heat so plants could be grown during cold weather.

Words to Know

Greenhouse effect:
The warming of Earth's atmosphere due to water vapor, carbon dioxide, and other gases in the atmosphere that trap heat radiated from Earth's surface.

Hypothesis:
An idea in the form of a statement that can be tested by observation and/or experiment.

These solar collectors turn to catch the Sun's rays throughout the day. (Photo Researchers Inc. Reproduced by permission.)

(W)ords to Know

Passive solar energy system:
A solar energy system in which the heat of the Sun is captured, used, and stored by means of the design of a building and the materials from which it is made.

Photoelectric effect:
The phenomenon in which light falling upon certain metals stimulates the emission of electrons and changes light into electricity.

Photovoltaic cells:
A device made of silicon that converts sunlight into electricity.

Solar collector:
A device that absorbs sunlight and collects solar heat.

Solar energy:
Any form of electromagnetic radiation that is emitted by the Sun.

Variable:
Something that can affect the results of an experiment.

Solar reflections

The Pyrenees Mountains, near Odeille in southern France, seem like an unlikely place for a solar reflector, but one has existed there since the 1950s. It towers over a meadow of wildflowers and features 63 separate mirrors that reflect sunlight onto a curved, mirrored wall. Electric motors move the mirrors to track sunlight and direct it to a central receiving tower. This method generates the intense heat needed for industrial use. It also produces steam in boilers, which is used to produce electricity.

Other solar energy collectors include **photovoltaic** (pronounced photo-vol-TAY-ic) cells, developed by three Bell Telephone scientists in 1954 as a way to produce electric power from sunlight. Also known as **solar cells,** they convert sunlight energy into electrical energy. They have been used to provide electric power during space exploration, but are most commonly used to light billboards and

This plant in the Pyrenees Mountains in France uses mirrors to capture solar energy. (Photo Researchers Inc. Reproduced by permission.)

power irrigation pumps. Because the energy output of solar cells is small, many are needed to produce a significant amount of electricity. However, newer cells now operate at about a 40 percent **efficiency,** a good rate compared to the efficiency of burning fossil fuels, which is about 34 percent.

In the experiment and project that follow, you will learn about two uses of solar energy: helping plants grow and powering electric motors. This experiment and project will help you appreciate all the ways that solar energy can—or could—affect our lives.

Experiment 1

Capturing Solar Energy: Will seedlings grow bigger in a greenhouse?

Purpose/Hypothesis

A greenhouse is a passive solar collector, allowing light energy to pass through while blocking the escape of heat. The locked-in heat and moisture from watering create a warm, humid environment similar to a rain forest. In this experiment, you will build a greenhouse and determine whether it helps seedlings grow faster and bigger. Clear plastic will be used as the walls of the greenhouse because it allows the light in and traps the heat.

To begin the experiment, use what you have learned about solar energy to make a guess about how the greenhouse will affect the seedlings. This educated guess, or prediction, is your **hypothesis.** A hypothesis should explain these things:

*   the topic of the experiment
*   the **variable** you will change
*   the variable you will measure
*   what you expect to happen

What Are the Variables?

Variables are anything that might affect the results of an experiment. Here are the main variables in this experiment:

*   the amount of sunlight reaching all the seedlings
*   the type of plants
*   the temperature outside the greenhouse
*   the color of the material under the greenhouse
*   the water and care given to the seedlings

In other words, the variables in this experiment are everything that might affect the growth of the seedlings. If you change more than one variable at a time, you will not be able to determine which variable had the most effect on the growth rate.

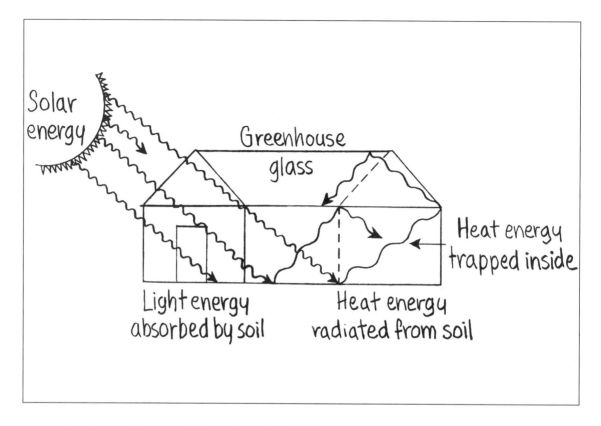

Greenhouse model.

A hypothesis should be brief, specific, and measurable. It must be something you can test through observation. Your experiment will prove or disprove whether your hypothesis is correct. Here is one possible hypothesis for this experiment: "The trapped solar energy in a greenhouse will cause seedlings to grow faster and larger than identical seedlings grown in the same environment without a greenhouse."

In this case, the variable you will change is whether seedlings are inside or outside the greenhouse, and the variable you will measure is the growth rate of the seedlings. If the seedlings inside the greenhouse grow more than those outside the greenhouse, your hypothesis is correct.

Level of Difficulty
Easy/moderate.

Materials Needed
- 4 wooden boards, roughly 1 x 6 x 20 inches (2.5 x 15 x 50 centimeters)
- 1 piece of transparent plastic or glass, 24 x 24-inch (60 x 60-centimeter) and 0.25 inch (0.5 centimeter) thick

- Eight 2-inch (5-centimeter) nails
- 10 marigold or radish seeds
- 10 small plastic pots, or 10 plastic yogurt containers, or 10 bottoms cut from 1-quart (1-liter) milk cartons
- soil
- hammer
- goggles
- gloves

Approximate Budget

$12. (Use any lumber that is cost-effective. When formed into a box, the lumber must be tall enough for the pots to fit under the glass or plastic and still have room for the seedlings to grow.)

Timetable

2 to 3 weeks. (This experiment requires 30 minutes to assemble the greenhouse and 2 to 3 weeks to monitor the plant growth.)

Step-by-Step Instructions

1. Hammer two nails through each end of a piece of wood, as illustrated. Repeat with a second piece of wood. Place the wood into a square with the two pieces with nails opposite each other.

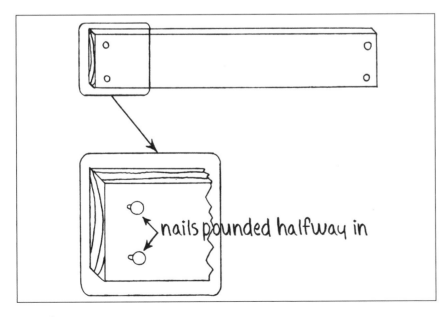

nails pounded halfway in

Step 1: Nails positioned on wood for assembling the greenhouse.

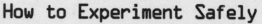

How to Experiment Safely

Goggles and adult supervision are required when hammering the nails. Wear gloves when handling the glass.

2. Hold the wood in position and assemble the box by carefully driving the nails into the ends of the two remaining pieces of wood.

3. Place the piece of plastic or glass over the wood box. Be sure it completely overlaps the wood box so there are no gaps around the edges.

Step 6: Growth chart for Experiment 1.

4. Place the greenhouse outside in a sunny spot or inside near a sunny window.

Growth Chart

Time	Seedlings in greenhouse	Seedlings outside greenhouse
3 days		
4 days		
5 days		
6 days		
7 days		
8 days		

experiment
CENTRAL

5. Plant the seedlings in the ten pots. Place five pots inside the greenhouse and five next to the greenhouse. Water each pot when the soil feels dry.

6. Measure and record the growth rate of each group of seedlings every day on a chart similar to the one illustrated. Continue your experiment for 2 weeks or longer.

Summary of Results

Study the results on your growth chart. Can you see a difference between the seedlings inside and outside the greenhouse? Which ones are grow-

Troubleshooter's Guide

Below are some problems that may arise during this experiment, some possible causes, and ways to remedy the problems.

Problem: The seedlings inside and outside the greenhouse are growing slowly.

Possible causes:

1. The time of year makes a difference, especially in the northern area of the country. During the winter, the Sun's rays are less intense, and all the seedlings will grow more slowly. You will still see a difference. It will just take a little more time.

2. The spot does not get enough sun. Move the greenhouse and the other seedlings to a sunnier spot.

3. There is a gap between the box and the glass or plastic, which allows the warm air and humidity inside the greenhouse to escape. Seal the gap with tape.

Problem: The seedlings inside the greenhouse withered and died after they sprouted.

Possible cause: During the summer, the temperature inside the greenhouse can soar to 110°F (43°C) or more in direct sun. Move the greenhouse and all ten pots to a less sunny location or cover the glass or plastic with a large sheet of thin white

ing faster? Which ones look healthier? Was your hypothesis correct? Did the heat and humidity in the greenhouse affect the plants' growth rate? Write a paragraph summarizing and explaining your findings.

Change the Variables

You can vary this experiment by using different kinds of seeds or using small, identical plants. You can also try growing plants under a "ceiling" of plastic, with the sides open to the air. Does this arrangement still trap enough heat to make a difference in the growth? Does the difference in humidity affect plant growth?

Project 2
Solar Cells: Will sunlight make a motor run?

Purpose

In this project, you will be working with photovoltaic cells, or solar cells, which utilize the **photoelectric effect** to convert solar energy into electricity. This project will allow you to determine if you can operate a small electric motor with solar cells. It will also let you determine how many cells and how much sunlight it takes to operate the motor.

Level of Difficulty

Easy/moderate.

Materials Needed

- 3 solar cells (.5-volt rating each)
- 1 DC motor (1.5-volt rating)
- 4 jumper wires with alligator clips on each end—three about 4 inches (10 centimeters) long, and one about 12 inches (30 centimeters) long
- stopwatch or clock
- marking pen
- posterboard or a small table to support the experiment
- cardboard to provide shade, about 24 inches (60 centimeters) square

Approximate Budget

$25. (Supplies can be purchased at an electronics store.)

Timetable

About 30 minutes.

How to Work Safely

Handle solar cells carefully. They are fragile and break easily.

Step-by-Step Instructions

1. Place the jumper wires with alligator clips on the + and - terminals of the solar cells, as illustrated. Attach the other ends to the motor terminal. Be careful to match the + or - connections. Place the experiment on a piece of posterboard or a small table so you can move it around.

2. Make a small mark on the shaft of the electric motor with the marking pen.

3. Test the ability of the solar cells to power the motor under different lighting conditions, such as the following:

   • outside on a sunny day
   • outside on a sunny day, but shaded by the cardboard
   • inside on a sunny day, but out of direct sunlight

Step 1: Set-up of three-cell circuit.

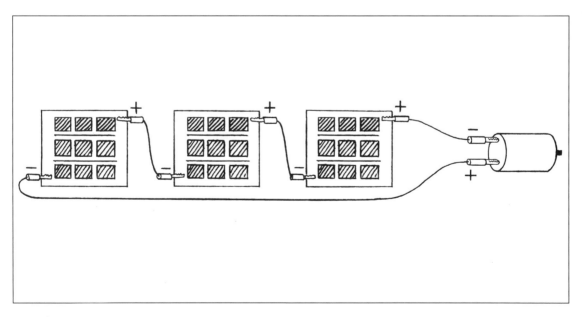

Performance Chart

Condition	Response
Outside on a sunny day	Number of rotations in 10 seconds: Other notes:
Inside on a sunny day	Number of rotations in 10 seconds: Other notes:

experiment
CENTRAL

Troubleshooter's Guide

Below is a problem that may arise during this project, a possible cause, and a way to remedy it.

Problem: The motor does not rotate under any condition.

Possible cause: The connections may be loose. Check them connections and try again.

- inside in a dark room
- inside at night under an incandescent and/or fluorescent light bulb

4. Record how many rotations the motor makes in 10 seconds—or if it runs at all—under each condition, using a chart similar to the one illustrated.

Summary of Results

Study your results. Under which conditions did the solar cells operate the motor? How many rotations could you record? Write a paragraph summarizing and explaining your findings.

Design Your Own Experiment

How to Select a Topic Relating to this Concept

First, define what aspect of solar energy you are interested in, such as ways to use this energy. You might want to investigate whether pollution is changing the effects of solar energy on our world.

Check the For More Information section and talk with your science teacher or school or community media specialist to start gathering information on solar energy questions that interest you. As you consider possible experiments, be sure to discuss them with a knowledgeable adult before trying them. Some of the materials or processes may be dangerous.

OPPOSITE PAGE:
Step 4: sample performance chart for Project 2.

Steps in the Scientific Method

To do an original experiment, you need to plan carefully and think things through. Otherwise you might not be sure which question you are answering, what you are or should be measuring, and what your findings prove or disprove.

Here are the steps in designing an experiment:

- State the purpose of—and the underlying question behind—the experiment you propose to do.
- Recognize the variables involved, and select one that will help you answer the question at hand.
- State a testable hypothesis, an educated guess about the answer to your question.
- Decide how to change the variable you selected.
- Decide how to measure your results

Recording and Summarizing the Results

Every good experiment should be documented so that other people can understand the procedures and results. Keep diagrams, charts, and graphs of any information that is useful. Your experiment, whether successful or not, is important information to be shared with others.

Related Projects

Solar energy is available on a daily basis (except on cloudy days), so take advantage of this free resource. For example, you could design and build a solar oven for cooking, a solar battery to run toys, or a radiometer to measure solar intensity. Explore the possibilities!

For More Information

Asimov, Issac. *The Sun and Its Secrets.* Milwaukee, WI: Gareth Stevens Publishing, 1994. ❖ Discusses the Sun's origins, content, and historical facts.

Edelson, Edward. *Clean Air.* New York: Chelsea House Publishers, 1992. ❖ Explores the devastating effects of population growth and industry on air quality and ways to clean up the air including using solar energy as a solution.

chapter 39

Sound

You hear sound when vibrations enter your ears and send signals through your nerves to your brain. These vibrations are caused by disturbances in the air. For example, when you hit a drum, the top of it vibrates, causing a disturbance in the molecules in the air. This vibration, or sound **wave,** travels through the air in all directions, eventually reaching your ears.

If you could see sound waves, they would look much like the waves you see when you drop a stone onto a calm water surface.

How do we hear?

Sound waves travel through air at about 1,088 feet (332 meters) per second. When the sound waves or vibrations reach your ears, they push on your eardrums and cause them to vibrate. Each eardrum pushes against a series of three tiny bones in your middle ear. These tiny bones push against another membrane, which causes waves in a fluid inside your inner ear. Here, special cells pick up the differences in pressure from the waves and transform them into electrical signals that travel along nerves to your brain. When these signals reach the brain, you hear the sound and usually recognize its source.

How is sound measured?

Sound waves are usually described with two measurements: **frequency** and **amplitude.** Frequency means the number of waves passing a given point in a given period of time. This is usually measured in **hertz,** abbreviated Hz. One hertz equals 1 cycle per second. Humans can usually hear sounds with frequencies from 20 Hz to 20,000 Hz. The

Words to Know

Acoustics:
The science concerned with the production, properties, and propagation of sound waves.

Amplitude:
The maximum displacement (difference between an original position and a later position) of the material that is vibrating. Amplitude can be thought of visually as the highest and lowest point of a wave.

Decibel (dB):
A unit of measurement for the amplitude of sound.

experiment
CENTRAL

As the drum vibrates, it pushes on molecules in the air, causing them to vibrate in the same way. This vibration, or sound wave, travels through the air in all directions, eventually reaching your ears. (Peter Arnold Inc. Reproduced by permission.)

ⓦords to Know

Frequency:
The rate at which vibrations take place (number of times per second the motion is repeated), given in cycles per second or in hertz (Hz). Also, the number of waves that pass a given point in a given period of time.

Hertz (Hz):
The unit of measurement of frequency; a measure of the number of waves that pass a given point per second of time.

Hypothesis:
An idea in the form of a statement that can be tested by observation and/or experiment.

Pitch:
A property of a sound, determined by its frequency; the highness or lowness of a sound.

Variable:
Something that can affect the results of an experiment

faster a wave vibrates, the higher its frequency and the higher a sound it produces. The highness or lowness of a sound is its **pitch.** A high-frequency sound has a high pitch.

The amplitude of the sound is its power or loudness. The taller the sound wave, the higher its amplitude and the louder the sound it produces. We usually measure amplitude in **decibels.** For example, leaves rustling in the wind might produce a sound of about 20 decibels, while a jet taking off creates a sound of at least 140 decibels, loud enough to damage your hearing. Listening to very loud sounds for a long time, including loud music, will damage the tiny nerves in your ears and can lead to a permanent hearing loss. Many rock musicians have discovered that they already have hearing problems.

How long have people wondered about sound?
People have been experimenting with sound for a long time. Pythagoras (572–497 B.C.) experimented with strings to determine

experiment
CENTRAL

Waves spread out from the source of the disturbance in wider and wider circles. (Grant Heilman. Reproduced by permission.)

how sounds changed with changes in the lengths of the strings. Historians credit him with the development of the musical scale.

In about 1700, French physicist Joseph Sauveur first used the word **acoustics** to describe music and the way sound works. He worked on the mathematics of sound and studied how strings made different sounds depending on their length.

Hermann von Helmholtz (1821–1894) discovered much about sound in the 1800s, especially the connections between mathematics and music. He also built one of the first sirens.

Sound, and the way humans and other animals perceive it, is a fascinating topic. What kind of questions do you have about sound? You will have an opportunity to explore different aspects of sound in the following experiments.

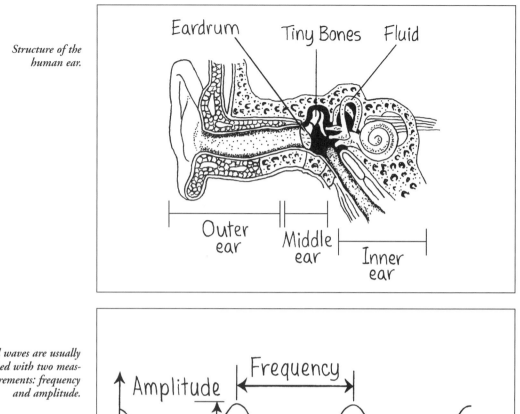

Structure of the human ear.

Eardrum Tiny Bones Fluid

Outer ear Middle ear Inner ear

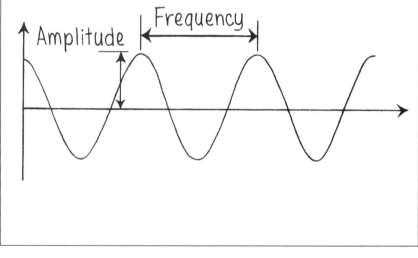

Sound waves are usually described with two measurements: frequency and amplitude.

Amplitude Frequency

Experiment 1
Wave Length: How does the length of a vibrating string affect the sound it produces?

Purpose/Hypothesis

In this experiment, you will find out how the length and tightness of a plucked string affects the sounds it produces. Before you begin, make

What Are the Variables?

Variables are anything that might affect the results of an experiment. Here are the main variables in this experiment:

- the kind of string
- the length of the string
- the tightness or tension of the string
- the strength with which the string is plucked
- the pitch of the sound
- the experimenter's ability to detect different pitches

In other words, the variables in this experiment are everything that might affect the perceived pitch of the sound. If you change more than one variable, you will not be able to tell which variable had the most effect on the pitch.

an educated guess about the outcome of the experiment based on your knowledge of sound. This educated guess, or prediction, is your **hypothesis.** A hypothesis should explain these things:

- the topic of the experiment
- the variable you will change
- the variable you will measure
- what you expect to happen

A hypothesis should be brief, specific, and measurable. It must be something you can test through observation. Your experiment will prove or disprove your hypothesis. Here is one possible hypothesis for this experiment: "The longer the string, the higher the pitch of the sound produced by that string."

In this case, the **variable** you will change will be the length of the string, and the variable you will measure will be the pitch of the sound. You expect a longer string to produce a higher pitch sound.

Level of Difficulty

Easy.

experiment
CENTRAL

How to Experiment Safely

Be careful handling the scissors.

Materials Needed

- a sturdy cardboard box, such as one for copy paper
- thin, strong string
- scissors
- hole-puncher
- ruler

Approximate Budget

$5, if you need to buy string; other materials should be available in the average household.

Timetable

1 hour.

Step-by-Step Instructions

You will be working with the top edge of two sides of the box; the edges join to make a V.

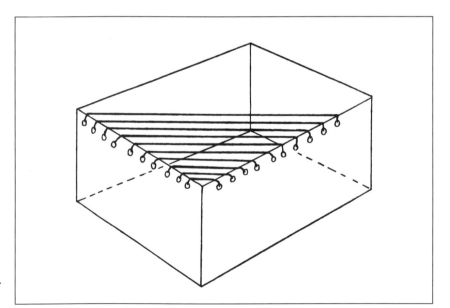

Steps 1 and 2: Set-up of experimental instrument.

String length	Sound produced
1 inch	
2 inches	

1. Use the hole puncher or the tip of your scissors to make ten small holes along each side of the V, placing the holes opposite from each other, as shown.

Step 3 and 6: Data sheet for Experiment 1.

2. Tie a length of string through each pair of holes, pulling it tightly before tying it to the other edge of the box. You should end up with strings of 10 lengths, as illustrated.

3. Using your ruler, measure the length of each string from knot to knot. Record these lengths on your data sheet.

4. Pluck each string several times and listen carefully. What do you hear? Describe it on your data sheet. You may want to play the strings for other people, so you are not depending on only your own ears.

5. If possible, bend the cardboard angle a little outward to pull the strings tighter and increase the tension. Repeat step 4. How do the sounds change?

Troubleshooter's Guide

Experiments do not always work out as planned. Even so, figuring out what went wrong can definitely be a learning experience. Here are some problems that may arise during this experiment, some possible causes, and ways to remedy the problems.

Problem: You cannot hear a clear sound from the strings.

Possible cause: Your strings are not tied tightly enough. Try again, trying them tightly.

Problem: All the strings sound the same.

Possible cause: Your cardboard box is not big enough to allow markedly different lengths of strings. Find a bigger box so the lengths of the strings vary more and try again.

6. Try plucking the strings harder and softer. Record what you hear on your data sheet.

Summary of Results

Study the results on your chart. Did the longer strings produce higher pitches or lower pitches? Why? Was your hypothesis correct? Did increasing the tension change the pitch of the sound? Write a paragraph summarizing and explaining what you have found.

Change the Variables

You can vary this experiment. Try using different materials, such as piano wire, fishing line, thicker string, or rubber bands. See how the pitch of the sound is affected.

Experiment 2
Pitch: How does the thickness of a vibrating string affect sound?

Purpose/Hypothesis

In this experiment, you will explore how the thickness of the vibrating object affects the pitches it produces. You will use different sizes of rubber bands to test this effect. Before you begin, make an educated guess about the outcome of this experiment based on your knowledge of sound. The educated guess, or prediction, is your **hypothesis.** A hypothesis should explain these things:

* the topic of the experiment
* the variable you will change
* the variable you will measure
* what you expect to happen

A hypothesis should be brief, specific, and measurable. It must be something you can test through observation. Your experiment will prove or disprove your hypothesis. Here is one possible hypothesis for this experiment: "Thicker bands will produce lower pitches."

In this case, the **variable** you will change will be the thickness of the rubber band, and the variable you will measure will be the pitch of the sound. You expect a thicker band to produce a lower pitch sound.

Level of Difficulty
Easy.

Materials Needed
* 8-inch- (20-centimeter-) square metal baking pan with straight sides
* 5 rubber bands of different thickness but the SAME length
* ruler

Approximate Budget
$5, if you need to purchase rubber bands; other materials should be available in the average household.

Timetable
1 hour.

Step-by-Step Instructions
1. Arrange the rubber bands in order from thinnest to thickest.

2. Measure the width of each rubber band with your ruler. Record these numbers on your data sheet, as illustrated on page 598.

3. Keep the bands in order, stretch each one over the pan, which acts as a sound box. Be sure to stretch them the same amount so the portion of the band over the open part of the pan is under the same tension as the rest of the band. See illustration on page 598.

Thickness of band	Sound produced
3 mm	
6 mm	
etc.	

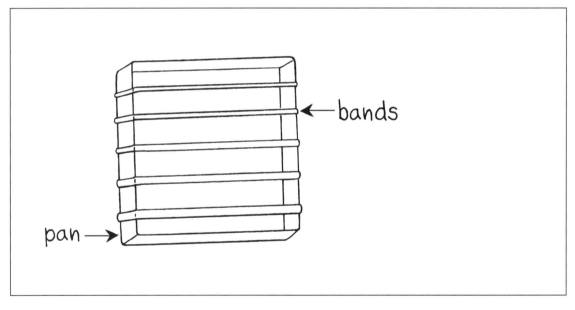

TOP: Step 2 and 5: Data sheet for Experiment 2.

BOTTOM: Step 3: Keeping the rubber bands in order, stretch each one over the pan, which acts as a sound box.

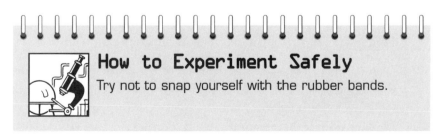

How to Experiment Safely

Try not to snap yourself with the rubber bands.

experiment
CENTRAL

Troubleshooter's Guide

Here are some problems that may arise during this experiment, some possible causes, and ways to remedy the problems.

Problem: You cannot hear the differences in the pitches.

Possible cause: Your rubber bands are too similar in size. Try to find bands that are several millimeters different in width. Check an office supply store or an art supply store.

Problem: You cannot hear much sound at all.

Possible cause: The pan is absorbing the vibrations. Be sure the pan is metal, with straight sides, and deep enough so the bands are free to vibrate.

4. Pluck each band, beginning with the thickest one, and listen carefully to the pitch it produces.

5. Describe each tone as you pluck the band and record on your data sheet what you hear.

Summary of Results

Study the results on your chart. How did the thickness of the band affect the pitch it produced? Did a thick band produce a lower pitch or a higher pitch? Thick bodies vibrate more slowly than small ones, and slower vibrations produce lower pitches. Is this what happened in your experiment? Was your hypothesis correct? Write a paragraph summarizing what you learned.

Change the Variables

You can vary this experiment in several ways. Try using bands with even greater differences in thickness. Record their width and see what happens. Try putting the same size bands on a larger pan and plucking the two instruments next to each other. What do you hear? Experiment with different size pans and you can create an entire orchestra. What is the effect of length on the sounds you produce? You can also use a box made from something else, such as wood or plastic. Repeat the experiment and record what you learn.

Design Your Own Experiment

How to Select a Topic Relating to this Concept

Are you interested in the frequency of vibrations and the pitches they produce, how to amplify sound to make it louder, or how to direct where the sound waves go? Maybe you are interested in how sound waves travel through different materials, such as gases, water, and solids. Would you like to make your own instruments and experiment with the sounds they make?

Check the For More Information section and talk with your science teacher or school or community media specialist to start gathering information about sound questions that interest you.

Steps in the Scientific Method

To do an original experiment, you need to plan carefully and think things through. Otherwise you may not be sure what question you are answering, what you are or should be measuring, or what your findings prove or disprove.

Here are the steps in designing an experiment:

*   State the purpose of—and underlying question behind—the experiment you propose to do.
*   Recognize the variables involved, and select one that will help you answer the question at hand.
*   State a testable hypothesis, an educated guess about the answer to your question.
*   Decide how to change the variable you selected.
*   Decide how to measure your results.

Recording Data and Summarizing the Results

Your data should include charts, such as the one you did for these experiments. They should be clearly labeled and easy to read. You may also want to include photos, graphs, or drawings of your experimental set-up and results.

If you are preparing an exhibit, display the sound-producing devices you create to help explain what you did and what you discovered. Observers could even test them out themselves. If you have done

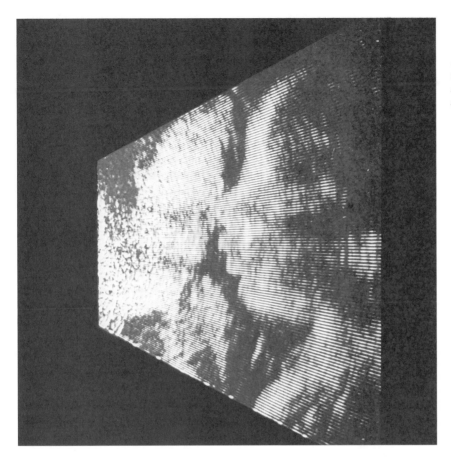

Ultrasound scan of a fetus. (Photo Researchers Inc. Reproduced by permission.)

a nonexperimental project, you will want to explain clearly what your research question was and illustrate your findings.

Related Projects

There are many uses of sound in modern technology. You could investigate how acoustics work in a large concert hall or how speakers and amplifiers work in your home sound system. You could also see how sound is used in modern medicine, in ultrasound machines, for example. These machines help doctors observe things that are difficult to see by turning sound into pictures.

For More Information

De Pinna, Simon, and Chris Fairclough. *Sound* (Science Projects). Austin, TX: Raintree/Steck Vaughn, 1998. ❖ Provides ideas for science fair projects involving the principles of sound.

Kaner, Etta. *Sound Science.* Toronto: Kids Can Press, 1991. ❖ Explores the nature of sound using games, puzzles, fun facts and experiments.

Van Cleave, Janice. *Physics for Every Kid: 101 Easy Experiments in Motion, Heat, Light, Machines, and Sound.* New York: John Wiley & Sons, 1991. ❖ Presents step-by-step experiments using household materials and scientific explanations.

experiment
CENTRAL

chapter 40

Stars

The first myth about the **stars** in the night sky probably came from the Chinese 5,000 years ago. They described stars as a heavenly river. The two brightest stars lived on either side of the river. They were known as Vega, a princess who wove beautiful clothes, and Altair, a herdsman. One night each year, a bridge of birds would span the river, allowing Vega and Altair to meet.

We now know that stars are not princesses, herdsmen, gods, or goddesses, but vast clumps of hydrogen gas and dust that exist in space millions of miles (kilometers) away. Scientists who study the positions, motions, and composition of stars, planets and other objects in space are known as **astronomers.**

What's up there?

Ancient people were intrigued by what we now call the **Milky Way.** What was this band of light that stretched across the skies, they wondered. According to Greek legend, droplets of milk spilt upwards when Juno breastfed the infant Hercules. That's why this light became known as the Milky Way.

Democritus, a Greek philosopher, realized the truth in the fifth century B.C. He suggested that countless stars, too faint to be seen individually, make up the Milky Way. In 1609, when the Italian astronomer Galileo Galilei (1564–1642) focused the telescope he had made, the immense number of stars he saw staggered him. Galileo confirmed that the Milky Way is made up of innumerable stars grouped in clusters.

Words to Know

Astronomers:
Scientists who study the positions, motions, and composition of stars and other objects in the sky.

Constellations:
Patterns of stars in the night sky. There are eighty-eight known constellations.

Fusion:
Combining of nuclei of two or more lighter elements into one nucleus of a heavier element; the process stars use to produce energy to produce light and support themselves against their own gravity.

experiment
CENTRAL

Galileo Galilei confirmed that a huge collection of stars make up the Milky Way. (Corbis Corp. Reproduced by permission.)

A star is born

How does a star begin? First, hydrogen, helium, dust, and ashes of stars that have died form swirling **nebula,** the Latin word for "cloud." When a dense accumulation of these nebula gathers, the mass becomes a spawning ground for stars. As this mass of gas and dust heats up, gravity causes it to clump together, and a new star is formed. But only after nuclear **fusion** takes place at the star's core does it produce enough light for us to see it. This process takes about 50 million years.

A star stays in the same spot during its lifetime. We do see stars in different positions over the course of a month, but this apparent movement of the stars is caused by Earth moving around the Sun. Certain stars lie in patterns called **constellations.** Of the eighty-eight constellation patterns, some form shapes that look like animals, women, warriors, or objects. Constellation patterns sparked the star myths told by ancient people.

Astronomers use **light-years** to measure the distance between stars. A light-year is the distance light travels in one year: roughly 5.9 trillion miles (9.5 trillion kilometers). How vast are the distances between stars? The star Proxima Centuri is 25 trillion miles (40 trillion kilometers) away—or 4.29 light-years. And that's the closest star.

The brightest and the biggest

Sirius, 8.6 light-years away, is the brightest star in the sky, twenty-six times brighter than the Sun, which is also a star. How was this determined? In 1912, astronomer Henrietta Swan Leavitt (1868–1921) discovered that stars increase and fade in brightness over time. By studying a sequence of photographs of stars, analyzing their changes, and

The Orion Nebula is the birthplace of at least 700 young stars. (Photo Researchers Inc. Reproduced by permission.)

Sirius is the brightest star in the sky. (Photo Researchers Inc. Reproduced by permission.)

applying mathematical formulas, Leavitt came up with a way for astronomers to calculate the true brightness of stars.

Stars are just one part of a **galaxy,** which also includes gas, dust, and planets, all drawn together by gravity. The Milky Way is not the only galaxy. The Andromeda Galaxy, which has about 300 trillion stars, and the Milky Way, with about 200 billion stars, are the two biggest and most important in a cluster of thirty galaxies called **The Local Group.** Currently, we know the universe contains about 100 billion galaxies.

The two projects that follow will help you learn more about the stars over our heads.

Project 1
Tracking Stars: Where is Polaris?

Purpose

Stars do not move in space, but the planets, including Earth, rotate on their axis and revolve around stars like our Sun. While stars appear to be in different places in the sky from one night to the next, what has really happened is that Earth has shifted its position.

In this project, you will use a camera to follow the stars. Normally when a picture is taken, the film is exposed to light for only a fraction of a second. In this experiment, the film will be exposed for 1200 seconds. To obtain a clear picture and avoid over-exposing the film, you must take the pictures at night in dark surroundings (no overhead lighting including street lights) with a clear sky and a view of the North Star (Polaris).

Level of Difficulty

Moderate, because of the camera operation.

Materials Needed

- single-lens reflex 35-mm manual camera, such as a Pentax K-1000 (your school may use this type in photography classes)
- 1 roll 35-mm film, 1000 speed, 12 to 24 exposures
- shutter bulb (Keeps the shutter open for prolonged exposures. You can purchase one in a photography store.)
- tripod stand for camera
- compass (optional)
- ruler and protractor

Approximate Budget

Less than $20 for film and shutter bulb. (Try to borrow all other supplies.)

Timetable

1 to 2 hours.

How to Work Safely

This project poses no hazards. However, you might ask a knowledgeable adult to help you operate the camera.

Step-by-Step Instructions

1. Properly load the film in the camera. If necessary, ask for help.

2. Set the shutter speed to the manual setting (M). Some cameras have a different symbol. Use the setting that keeps the shutter open as long as you press the shutter button.

3. Set the film speed at 1000.

4. Attach the shutter bulb by screwing the end into the shutter button.

5. Set the aperture to the highest number.

6. Screw the tripod into the bottom of the camera

Steps 2 to 5: Parts of a camera.

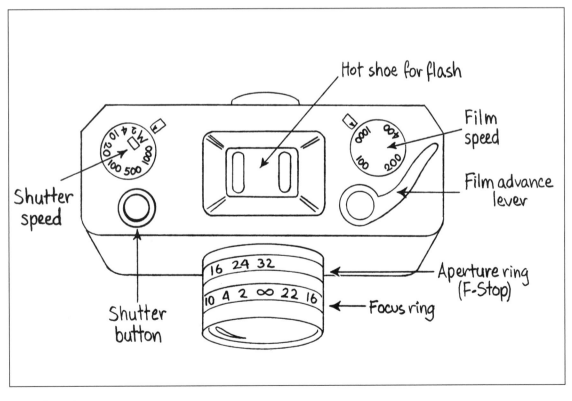

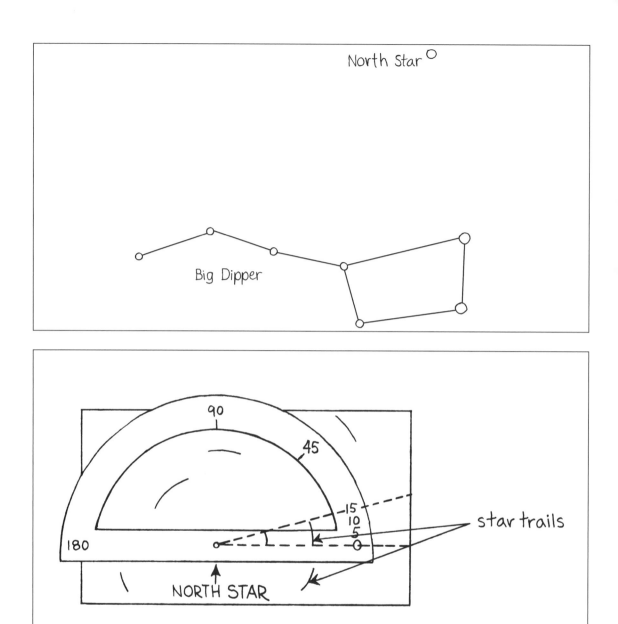

TOP: Step 8: Locate Polaris, the North Star, in the northern sky, using the pointer stars of the Big Dipper.

BOTTOM: Step 16: Compass over photo with lines drawn to North Star from an angle.

7. Set the tripod on firm ground.

8. Locate Polaris, the North Star, in the northern sky, using the pointer stars of the Big Dipper.

9. Position the camera so the North Star is visible through the eyepiece.

10. Squeeze the bulb to open the shutter. Hold it open by adjusting the screw near the bulb.

experiment
CENTRAL

Troubleshooter's Guide

Here is a problem that may arise during this project, some possible causes, and ways to remedy the problem.

Problem: The photo is too hazy, and the star trails are not visible.

Possible causes: The sky was not clear enough, or there were too many lights that overexposed the film. Try the project again, away from houses and streets.

11. Leave the shutter open for 1 hour.

12. Close the shutter by loosening the screw or releasing the bulb.

13. Advance the film and repeat steps 10 through 12 on different nights.

14. Remove the roll of film and get it developed.

15. Using a pen, draw lines on each photo from the North Star (the only star that did not move) to the ends of one or two star trails.

16. Using a compass, measure the angle of the two lines. The angle should measure 15 degrees for each hour the film is exposed.

Summary of Results

Record your angle measurements and the date on each photo. All angles should be 15 degrees for each hour of exposure because Earth revolves 15 degrees each hour. What seemed to happen to all the stars except the North Star? How can you explain this?

Project 2
Tracking the Motion of the Planets: Can a planet be followed?

Purpose

Planets sometimes reflect light from the Sun, which makes them shine like stars. But unlike the stationary stars, Earth and the other planets move through the sky as they orbit the Sun. As the other planets orbit the Sun, Earth continues through its orbit. The combination of these movements can make the apparent path of the planets in Earth's sky resemble an s-shaped pattern. In this project, you will examine this phenomenon.

Level of Difficulty

Moderate. (You need to be familiar with the star positions.)

Materials Needed

- a star map for your area and time of the year
- binoculars or telescope (optional)

Approximate Budget

$2 for a star map. (Consult local papers or magazines for current monthly maps.)

Timetable

15 to 20 minutes per night for 10 to 15 nights.

Step-by-Step Instructions

1. Examine your local star map. Most star maps should be held upside down and over your head.

2. Choose a planet that should be visible in your night sky. Locate its position on the map.

3. With or without using binoculars, try to find this planet in the night sky. Planets are usually the brightest objects in the sky and do not twinkle like stars.

4. On your star map, record the position and time you located the planet.

5. Repeat this procedure every night for 10 to 15 nights.

6. Connect the marks on the star map and trace the path of the planet.

OPPOSITE PAGE TOP: Steps 3 to 5: Example of plotting the position of a planet on Day 1 and 2, related to the Orion Constellation.

OPPOSITE PAGE BOTTOM: Step 6: Example of graphing a planet's motion relative to the Orion Constellation.

How to Work Safely

Always stay on level ground when star gazing. Have an adult with you.

experiment
CENTRAL

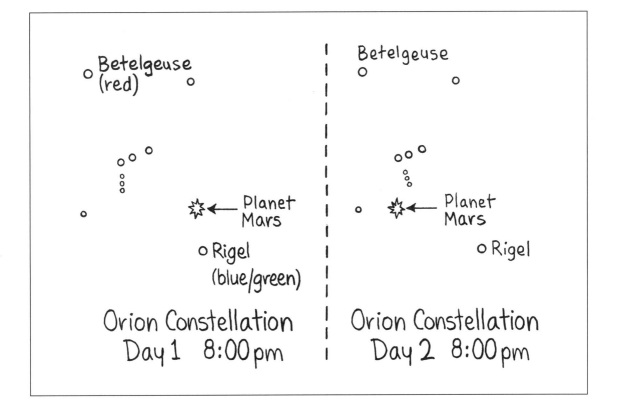

Betelgeuse (red)

Planet Mars

Rigel (blue/green)

Orion Constellation
Day 1   8:00 pm

Betelgeuse

Planet Mars

Rigel

Orion Constellation
Day 2   8:00 pm

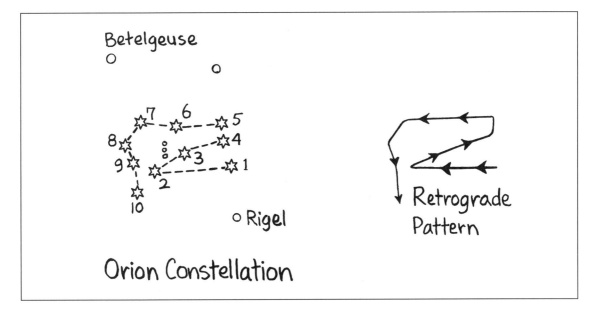

Betelgeuse

Orion Constellation

Rigel

Retrograde Pattern

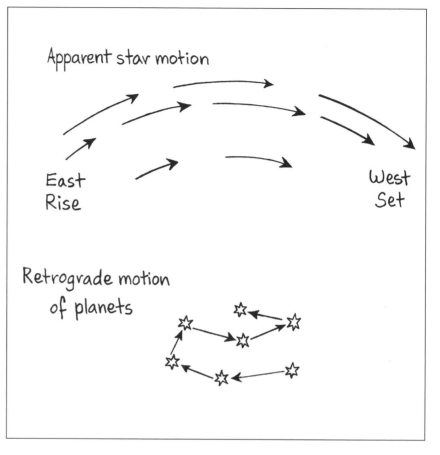

Apparent star motion

East
Rise

West
Set

Retrograde motion
of planets

Troubleshooter's Guide

Here are some problems that may arise during this project, some possible causes, and ways to remedy the problems.

Problem: You cannot see the planets or stars.

Possible cause: The sky is too overcast. Try coming out again an hour or two later.

Problem: You cannot find the new position of the planet.

Possible cause: You might be unfamiliar with the night sky. Ask a knowledgeable adult for help, or look on the Internet for a daily star map. Locate the planet and transfer its position to your star map.

Summary of Results

Record your results on a star map like the one illustrated on page 612. Be sure to label each star and the daily positions of the planet. After 10 to 15 nights of observations, were you able to notice the motion of the planet among the stars?

Design Your Own Experiment

How to Select a Topic Relating to this Concept

Space is an infinite frontier sparsely filled with objects. Comets, stars, meteors, asteroids, moons, and planets are just a few of the objects visible in space. Before you begin making observations or experimenting, ask yourself questions. What is an asteroid? What is the difference between a meteor and a meteorite?

Check the For More Information section and talk with your science teacher or school or community media specialist to start gathering information on star questions that interest you.

Steps in the Scientific Method

To do an original experiment, you need to plan carefully and think things through. Otherwise, you might not be sure what question you are answering, what you are or should be measuring, or what your findings prove or disprove.

Here are the steps in designing an experiment:

- State the purpose of—and the underlying question behind—the experiment you propose to do.
- State a testable hypothesis, an educated guess about the answer to your question.
- Decide how to change the variable you selected.
- Decide how to measure your results.

Recording Data and Summarizing the Results

As a scientist investigating a question, you must gather information and share it with others. Observations, researched facts, and data can be diagrammed or charted. Once you have gathered your information, study it, draw a conclusion, and share your results with others.

Related Projects

Binoculars and telescopes can improve your view of the nighttime sky. When choosing a topic such as comets, make sure you have the proper instruments to observe the object. You may want to choose a phenomenon or event that is easily observed, such as a meteor shower. When a meteor shower is predicted, you might try to calculate the number of shooting stars you see in one hour.

For More Information

Matloff, Gregory L. *The Urban Astronomer.* New York: John Wiley, 1991. ❖ Describes interesting objects you can see in a city sky.

McSween, Jr,. Harry Y. *Stardust to Planets.* New York: St. Martin's Press, 1993. ❖ Provides a good survey of the solar system.

Van Cleave, Janice. *Astronomy for Every Kid.* New York: John Wiley, 1991. ❖ Outlines more than one hundred simple experiments that demonstrate the principles of astronomy.

chapter 41

Static Electricity

You experiment with static electricity every time you shuffle across a rug and touch a metal door handle. **Static electricity** is a form of electricity produced by **friction** (the rubbing of one object against another) in which the electric charge does not flow in a **current** but stays in one place.

Electricity is a form of energy caused by the presence of electrical charges in matter. **Matter** is anything that has mass and takes up space. All matter, including you and this book, is made of tiny particles called atoms. An **atom** is the smallest particle of which an element can exist. Each atom, in turn, contains positively charged **protons** in its **nucleus**, or center core, and negatively charged **electrons** orbiting around its nucleus.

How does an object become electrically charged?

An increase or decrease in the number of electrons in an object gives it an electrical charge. When an object gains electrons, it becomes negatively charged. When it loses electrons, it becomes positively charged.

In some materials, such as copper and silver, electrons can move around freely. These "free" electrons make these two metals good conductors. A **conductor** is a substance that is able to carry an electrical current. In other materials, electrons are tightly bound to their atoms. These materials, such as glass, rubber, and dry wood, do not conduct electricity easily, so they are good **insulators** and can be used as protective layers around conductors.

Some materials have a stronger attraction for electrons than other materials. When two different materials are rubbed together, electrons

Words to Know

Atom:
The smallest unit of an element, made up of protons and neutrons in a central nucleus surrounded by moving electrons.

Conductor:
A substance able to carry an electrical current.

Control experiment:
A setup that is identical to the experiment but is not affected by the variable that will be changed during the experiment.

Rubbing does not create new electrons. It just causes them to move from the paper to the balloon.

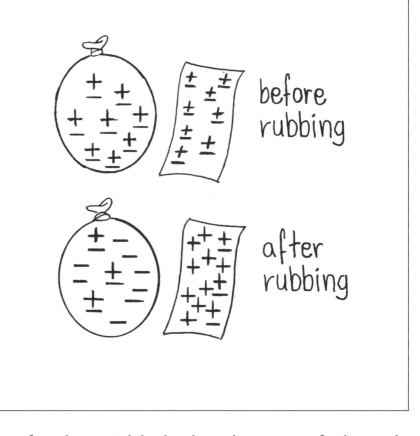

before rubbing

after rubbing

move from the material that has the weaker attraction for them to the material that has the stronger attraction. For example, a balloon will usually not stick to a sheet of paper. However, you can make it stick by rubbing them together. As you rub, electrons move from the paper, which has a weak attraction for electrons, to the balloon, which has a stronger attraction. Because the paper has lost some electrons, it now is positively charged. The balloon has gained electrons, so it is now negatively charged.

When it comes to electrical charges, opposites attract. A material with a positive charge attracts a material with a negative charge, and vice versa. However, materials that both have a positive charge repel (are resistant to) each other, as do materials that both have a negative charge.

When you place the negatively charged balloon near the positively charged paper, they will now cling together. As they cling, however, some of the electrons move from the balloon back to the paper. When

the electrons are evenly distributed again, the balloon and paper are no longer electrically charged, so they will stop clinging together.

What is static electricity?

As you placed the charged balloon near the charged paper, you might have seen or heard a small crackle of static electricity. When an object with a strong negative charge is placed near one with a strong positive charge, the attraction of these opposites is so great that the air between them becomes electrically charged. It forms a path over which the electrons can move. As the electrons jump from the negative object to the positive one, they create static electricity. After the jump, the electrons are balanced again, so both objects lose their electrical charge.

American scientist and political leader Benjamin Franklin (1706–1790) was one of the first to experiment with static electricity. You may remember his famous and dangerous kite experiments with lightning, which is a form of static electricity.

Benjamin Franklin was the first to use the words "positive" and "negative" to describe electric charges. (Photo Researchers Inc. Reproduced by permission.)

ⓦords to Know

Matter:
Anything that has mass and takes up space.

Nucleus:
The central core of an atom, consisting of protons and (usually) neutrons.

experiment
CENTRAL

Lightning is a form of static electricity. (Peter Arnold Inc. Reproduced by permission.)

(W)ords to Know

Proton:
A subatomic particle with a single positive charge that is found in the nucleus of an atom.

Static electricity:
A form of electricity produced by friction in which the electric charge does not flow in a current but stays in one place.

Variable:
Something that can affect the results of an experiment.

Scientists still do not know exactly how lightning occurs, but they do know that a negative charge in one cloud repels electrons on the ground beneath it or in another cloud. As these electrons are repelled, the surface of the ground or the other cloud facing the negative cloud ends up with an excess of protons, giving it a positive charge. When the difference between the negative and positive charges reaches a certain point, lightning flashes from the negatively charged cloud to the positively charged ground or to the other cloud. This powerful burst of static electricity balances the electrons at both locations.

In the first experiment, you will build an **electroscope,** a device that determines whether an object is electrically charged, and you will use it to test objects for electrical charges. In the second experiment, you will determine whether wool or nylon creates a stronger electrical charge.

Experiment 1
Building an Electroscope: Which objects are electrically charged?

Purpose/Hypothesis
In this experiment, you will build an electroscope and use it to determine whether objects have an electric charge. An electroscope has two metal strips that hang down. When you hold a negatively charged object near the strips, the excess electrons move into the strips, causing them both to have a negative charge. Because they both have the same charge, they will repel each other and move apart. When you remove the charged object, the strips will lose their negative charge and hang down, as before.

An electroscope responds in the same way if a positively charged object is brought near the strips. The positively charged object attracts electrons from the strips, giving them both a positive charge. This time the strips move apart because they are both positively charged.

Before you begin, make an educated guess about the outcome of this experiment based on your knowledge of static electricity. This educated guess, or prediction, is your **hypothesis.** A hypothesis should explain these things:

*   the topic of the experiment
*   the variable you will change

An electroscope can determine whether an object holds an electric charge. *(Peter Arnold Inc. Reproduced by permission.)*

- the variable you will measure
- what you expect to happen

A hypothesis should be brief, specific, and measurable. It must be something you can test through observation. Your experiment will prove or disprove whether your hypothesis is correct. Here is one possible hypothesis for this experiment: "A glass test tube and a plastic comb that have been rubbed will hold an electric charge, but identical objects that have not been rubbed will not hold a charge."

In this case, the **variable** you will change is whether the objects have been rubbed, and the variable you will measure, using the electroscope, is the electric charge of the objects. You expect the objects to have a charge only after they have been rubbed.

The unrubbed objects will serve as a **control experiment,** showing whether the objects have an electric charge if they have not been

experiment
CENTRAL

What Are the Variables?

Variables are anything that might affect the results of an experiment. Here are the main variables in this experiment:

- whether the experimental and control objects are identical
- which objects are rubbed
- how long and in what manner the objects are rubbed
- whether the test objects touch each other (keep those you rubbed—the experimental objects—separate from those you did not rub—the control objects—so electrons will not move from one to the other before you test them)
- the humidity level of the air (electric charges can leak away in humid air and change the results of your experiment)

In other words, the variables in this experiment are everything that might affect the electric charges of the objects. If you change more than one variable, you will not be able to tell which variable had the most effect on each object's electric charge.

rubbed. If only the rubbed objects have an electric charge, you will know your hypothesis is correct.

Level of Difficulty

Easy/moderate.

Materials Needed

- 1 wide-mouth jar
- cardboard circle cut to cover the jar opening
- 2 strips of aluminum foil, each 0.5 inches x 2 inches (1.3 centimeters x 5 centimeters)
- large paper clip
- sharpened pencil
- masking tape
- scissors

How to Experiment Safely

Be careful in handling the glass materials and in using the scissors.

- clean, dry cloth
- 2 identical pairs of objects to test, such as two glass test tubes and two plastic combs

Approximate Budget

$0 to $5. The materials should be available in most households.

Timetable

15 minutes to build the electroscope; 10 minutes to test the objects.

Step-by-Step Instructions

1. Choose a day with low humidity to do your experiment. (If the air feels damp, it has just rained, or you seem to perspire easily, the humidity is too high for this experiment.)

2. Use the pencil to make a small hole in one end of each foil strip.

3. Open the paper clip so that it becomes a loop with two hooks at the bottom.

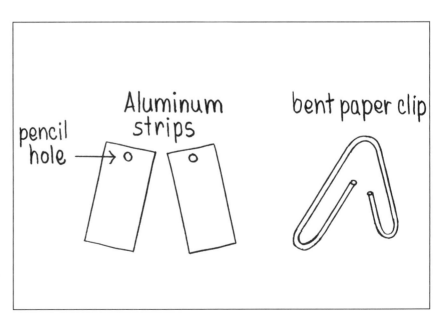

Steps 2 and 3: Preparing aluminum foil strip and paper clip.

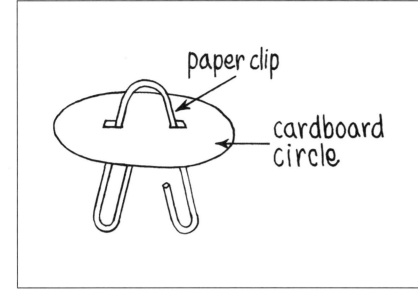

Step 4: Set-up of cardboard circle and paper clip.

Step 8: Recording chart for Experiment 1.

Reaction Chart

Control Object 1	Reaction of aluminum strips:
Control Object 2	Reaction of aluminum strips:
Experimental (rubbed) Object 1	Reaction of aluminum strips:
Experimental (rubbed) Object 2	Reaction of aluminum strips:

4. Use the scissors to cut two slots in the cardboard circle. Slip the sides of the paper clip into the slots.

5. Hang each foil strip on a paper clip hook. If the strips do not move freely, enlarge the holes in them.

6. Use masking tape to secure the cardboard circle to the top of the jar. Your electroscope is ready to use.

7. Hold one of the control objects near the top of the paper clip loop that is sticking out of the cardboard circle. Do not touch the clip with the object.

8. Move the object away. Use a chart such as the one illustrated on page 623 to record whether the aluminum strips moved apart.

9. Repeat Steps 7 and 8 with the other control object.

10. Rub one test object vigorously with the dry cloth and repeat Steps 7 and 8.

Troubleshooter's Guide

Below are some problems that may arise during this experiment, some possible causes, and ways to remedy the problems.

Problem: The aluminum strips did not move for any objects.

Possible causes:

1. The air is too humid. Wait for a drier day and try again.

2. The holes in the strips are too small, preventing movement. Enlarge the holes and try again.

3. The test objects were not charged. Rub them longer or try rubbing them with a wool scarf.

Problem: The strips moved for all of the objects.

Possible cause: The control objects were charged accidentally. Touch them to something metal to release any electric charge in them and test them again.

11. Rub the other test object vigorously with the cloth and repeat Steps 7 and 8.

Summary of Results

Use the data on your chart to create a line or bar graph of your findings. Then study your chart and graph and decide whether your hypothesis was correct. Did the aluminum strips move apart only for the rubbed objects? What does this show? Write a paragraph summarizing your findings and explaining whether they support your hypothesis.

Change the Variables

You can vary this experiment in several ways. For example, use different pairs of objects, including copper or silver objects that are good conductors. You can also put an object that you know has a positive charge near the paper clip. For example, you might use paper after it has been rubbed against a balloon. Do the aluminum strips respond in the same way?

Experiment 2
Measuring a Charge: Does nylon or wool create a stronger static electric charge?

Purpose/Hypothesis

In this experiment, you will create an electric charge in nylon, which is a synthetic fiber, and in wool, a natural fiber. Then you will measure the strength of each charge, using the electroscope you built in Experiment 1 or using an alternative procedure.

Before you begin, make an educated guess about the outcome of this experiment based on your understanding of static electricity. This educated guess, or prediction, is your **hypothesis.** A hypothesis should explain these things:

- the topic of the experiment
- the variable you will change
- the variable you will measure
- what you expect to happen

What Are the Variables?

Variables are anything that might affect the results of an experiment. Here are the main variables in this experiment:

- the types of cloth used and the size of the pieces
- whether the pairs of control and experimental cloth squares are identical
- which cloth squares are rubbed
- how long the cloth squares are rubbed and what they are rubbed against
- whether the rubbed cloth squares touch anything before they are tested
- the humidity level of the air (electric charges can leak away in humid air and change the results of your experiment)

In other words, the variables in this experiment are everything that might affect the strength of the static electric charge. If you change more than one variable, you will not be able to tell which one had the most effect on the strength of the static charge.

A hypothesis should be brief, specific, and measurable. It must be something you can test through observation. Your experiment will prove or disprove whether your hypothesis is correct. Here is one possible hypothesis for this experiment: "Wool will create a stronger static electric charge than nylon."

In this case, the **variable** you will change is the material being rubbed, and the variable you will measure is the strength of the electrostatic charge, as measured on your electroscope. You expect the wool will have a stronger charge.

As a control experiment, you will also test squares of wool and nylon that have not been rubbed. The control experiment will determine whether these unrubbed cloth squares also have a charge and, if so, how strong it is. If the rubbed wool has a stronger charge than the

experiment
CENTRAL

rubbed nylon and if the unrubbed cloth squares have little or no static charge, you will know your hypothesis is correct.

Level of Difficulty
Easy/moderate.

Materials Needed
- two 5-inch (12.7-centimeter) squares of wool
- two 5-inch (12.7-centimeter) squares of nylon
- plastic comb
- electroscope from Experiment 1 (or a clean, empty margarine tub with a clear lid and some dry, lightweight cereal, such as puffed rice)
- ruler

Approximate Budget
$3 for cloth. (The other materials should be available in most households.)

Timetable
20 minutes.

Step-by-Step Instructions
To use an electroscope to measure the strength of a static charge:

1. Choose a dry day to do your experiment. Be careful not to rub the control squares of cloth against anything.

2. Place the control wool square near the paper clip loop. Observe the response of the aluminum strips. If they move, use the ruler to estimate the distance between the lower edges of the two strips. Record the results on a chart like the one illustrated on page 628.

3. Repeat Step 2 with the control nylon square.

4. Rub the experimental wool square vigorously against the comb. Then, without touching the cloth to anything, hold it near the paper clip loop. Observe and record how the aluminum strips respond.

5. Repeat Step 4 using the experimental nylon square, rubbing it in the same way and as long as you rubbed the wool square.

   To use an alternative testing procedure:

Chart of Reactions

Control wool square	Reaction of aluminum strips:	Width between bottom of strips:
Control nylon square	Reaction of aluminum strips:	Width between bottom of strips:
Experimental (rubbed) wool square	Reaction of aluminum strips:	Width between bottom of strips:
Experimental (rubbed) nylon square	Reaction of aluminum strips:	Width between bottom of strips:

Step 2: Recording chart for Experiment 2.

Rubbing a plastic margarine container with a cloth square will give the container a static electric charge that will draw lightweight cereal toward the container. Rubbing causes electrons to leave the cloth and move to the plastic tub. The negatively charged tub then repels the electrons in the cereal and attracts the protons, drawing the cereal upward.

1. Choose a day with low humidity for your experiment.

2. Place about 15 pieces of cereal in the tub lid.

3. As a control experiment, hold the empty margarine container about 1 inch (2.5 centimeters) above the lid of cereal. Observe whether any cereal pieces move upward toward the bottom of the container, and record your findings on a chart.

4. With one hand inside the container, rub the outside vigorously

experiment
CENTRAL

with a square of wool. Then remove the wool and hold the container above the cereal. Record how the cereal pieces respond and how many respond.

5. Repeat Step 4 with the nylon square, rubbing in the same way and for the same length of time. Record the results.

Step 3: Hold an empty margarine container about 1 inch (2.5 centimeters) above the lid of cereal.

Summary of Results

Use the data on your charts to create a line or bar graph of your findings. Then study your charts and graph and decide whether your hypothesis was correct. Did the wool square create more static electricity than the nylon square, either causing the aluminum strips to move farther apart or causing more cereal to cling to the bottom of the margarine container? Did the unrubbed cloth squares exert no noticeable static charge, according to your electroscope? Or did the unrubbed container not pull the cereal upward? Write a paragraph summarizing your findings and explaining whether they support your hypothesis.

Change the Variables

You can change the variables and conduct other interesting experiments. For example, use different kinds of synthetic and natural fabrics, such as rayon, polyester knit, cotton, or silk. You can also change the length of time you rub a cloth square to see if the strength of the electric charge increases the longer you rub.

Another way to vary the experiment is to rub a cloth square against the plastic comb, and hold the comb near the paper clip in the electroscope instead of the cloth. The comb should also hold a static charge, although it will be negative, while the cloth should be positive.

Troubleshooter's Guide

Below are some problems that may arise during this experiment, some possible causes, and ways to remedy the problems.

Problem: None of the cloth squares held a static charge.

Possible causes:

1. The air is too humid. Wait for a drier day and try again.

2. The experimental squares were not charged. Rub them longer, making sure to rub both kinds of cloth in the same way.

Problem: All of the cloth squares held a charge.

Possible cause: The control squares might have been charged accidentally as you prepared for your experiment. Touch them to something metal to release any electric charge in them and test them again.

Problem: The pieces of cereal flew all around.

Possible cause: The cereal had already been charged, perhaps by being shaken and rubbed inside the box. Try a different box of cereal and try not to let the pieces rub together.

(The electroscope should respond in the same way because both aluminum strips will still receive the same kind of charge and move apart.)

Instead of using cereal in the alternative electroscope design, you can put salt and pepper or tiny pieces of paper in the margarine container.

Design Your Own Experiment

How to Select a Topic Relating to this Concept

You can explore many other aspects of static electricity. For example, why does static electricity occur in some situations and not in others?

What kinds of materials are more likely to have a positive or a negative charge? How does the humidity in the air affect static electricity? How do static charges affect electrical equipment?

As you consider possible experiments, be sure to discuss them with your science teacher or another knowledgeable adult before trying them. While static electricity usually involves a small electric charge (except for lightning!), experiments with electricity are potentially dangerous. NEVER experiment with lightning or the electric current that comes from electrical outlets.

Check the For More Information section and talk with your science teacher or school or community media specialist to start gathering information on static electricity questions that interest you.

Steps in the Scientific Method

To do an original experiment, you need to plan carefully and think things through. Otherwise, you might not be sure what question you are answering, what you are or should be measuring, or what your findings prove or disprove.

Here are the steps in designing an experiment:

- State the purpose of—and the underlying question behind—the experiment you propose to do.
- Recognize the variables involved, and select one that will help you answer the question at hand.
- State a testable hypothesis, an educated guess about the answer to your question.
- Decide how to change the variable you selected.
- Decide how to measure your results.

Recording Data and Summarizing the Results

In the static electricity experiments, your raw data might include not only charts and graphs of the responses of control and electrically charged objects, but also drawings or photographs of these responses.

If you display your experiment, make clear your beginning question, the variable you changed, the variable you measured, the results, and your conclusions. You might include photographs or drawings of the steps of the experiment. Explain what materials you used, how long each step took, and other basic information.

Related Projects

You can undertake a variety of projects related to static electricity. For example, you might explore products that claim to stop static cling on clothes. Does one product work better than another? You might see how many times you can transfer a static charge from one object to another, or if you can use static electricity to move objects without touching them.

For More Information

Bonnet, Robert. *Science Fair Projects with Electricity and Electronics.* New York: Sterling Publishing, 1996. ❖ Outlines nearly fifty projects designed for science fairs.

Garner, Robert. *Science Projects about Electricity and Magnets.* Hillside, NJ: Enslow Publishers, 1994. ❖ Provides detailed explanations of projects and the concepts they demonstrate.

Gibson, Gary. *Understanding Electricity.* Brookfield, CT: Copper Beech Books, 1995. ❖ Explains basic concepts and includes experiments.

VanCleave, Janice. *Spectacular Science Projects: Electricity.* New York: Wiley & Sons, 1994. ❖ Describes twenty science projects, explaining how to carry them out and what they prove.

Wood, Robert. *Electricity and Magnetism FUNdamentals.* New York: Learning Triangle Press, 1997. ❖ Offers instructions for experiments on the nature of electricity and magnetism and the relationship between them.

chapter 42

Structures and Shapes

Humans have been busy building structures for almost as long as we have existed. The structures that we build, however, have changed dramatically over the last thousand years. We have learned to construct buildings that extend thousands of feet up, and we can build bridges that safely support tons of weight over immense stretches of water. What have we learned that enables us to build what our ancestors would have thought impossible?

The answer lies mainly in concepts about the nature of force and motion that Sir Isaac Newton (1642–1727) developed over three hundred years ago. Newton proposed a set of "laws" that clearly explain why and how objects move or remain still. These laws apply to the planning of structures like buildings and bridges because they must be designed to remain fixed in place and not be moved by the forces that act upon them.

Different forces can act upon one object

One of Newton's laws tells us that different forces can act on a single object at the same time, as when two soccer players kick the ball at the same time. One has exerted force on the ball toward the goal; the other has exerted force in another direction. If the two players kick with precisely the same energy in exactly opposite directions, then the ball will remain motionless. Two kicks that are not equal in energy and not opposite in direction, however, will send the ball flying sideways off the field. This combined force is called a **resultant**.

Standing a single playing card on its edge is nearly impossible. Two cards, however, can be stood on edge quite easily. This is because the

Words to Know

Arch:
A curved structure that spans an opening and supports a weight above the opening.

Beam:
A straight, horizontal structure that spans an opening and supports a weight above the opening.

Compression:
A type of force on an object where the object is pushed or squeezed from each end.

Equilibrium:
A balancing or canceling out of opposing forces, so that an object will remain at rest.

A card house can stand because the forces acting on it add up to a resultant of zero. (Corbis-Bettmann. Reproduced by permission.)

two cards can be made to exert two equal and exactly opposite forces upon each other. As long as this force stays balanced, the cards will remain standing. When different forces add up to a resultant of zero, this state is called **equilibrium.** If you increase the force on one side without increasing the force on the other, the resultant is no longer zero; equilibrium has been disrupted, and the cards will fall in the direction exerted by the stronger force.

The science of architecture and engineering is largely the analysis of force: how to distribute and direct the many forces acting on a structure to ensure that it remains in equilibrium.

The arch redistributes forces to maintain equilibrium

One early development in architecture that uses the principle of distribution of force is the **arch.** The arch directs the downward force of the supported weight around the arch and into the ground. In a

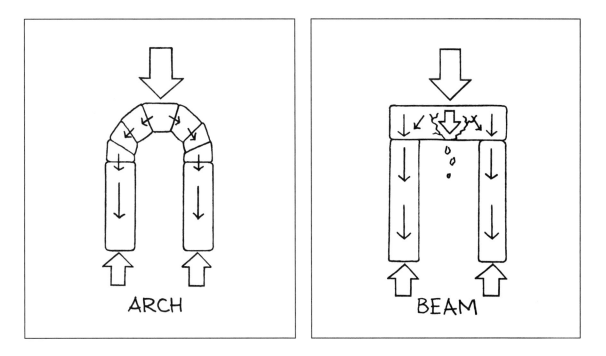

ARCH

BEAM

stone arch, for example, each stone has slightly tapered sides. The weight on the top stone causes it to push out and down on the next stone, and so on around the curve of the arch until it reaches the ground. An arch can support greater weight than a straight **beam** across an opening, even when the beam and arch are built of the same materials. This is because the force in an arch squeezes, or compresses, the material in the arch, rather than bending it the way it does in a beam. Most materials are stronger in **compression** than they are in bending. The greatest bending force in a beam takes place in the center, where it is unsupported. Over time, the bending force on the beam could cause it to crack.

The same principle applies to bridges. The **platform** of a bridge, the flat surface over which vehicles travel, can be supported either by a beam or by an arch. A simple beam bridge can extend only a limited distance before its weight and the weight of the traffic upon it would cause the beam to fail. An arch bridge more effectively transfers the force of this weight out to the ground. Many large bridges today use arches as part of their design.

In the first project, you will construct two bridges—one using a beam and one using an arch—and determine whether the arch can support more weight. In the second project, you will see if you can

LEFT: The arch is an effective design because it distributes the downward force around the arch and into the ground.

RIGHT: The beam design is limited in the weight it can bear because the middle section is unsupported.

increase the strength of the beam design by increasing the vertical height of the beam.

Project 1
Arches and Beams: Which is strongest?

Purpose
In this project, you will construct one bridge using an arch and one using a beam. The bridges will use the same vertical supports and platforms, and the arch and beam will be of identical thickness. You will test the bridges to determine how much weight each one can support.

Level of Difficulty
Easy/moderate.

Materials Needed
- 1 sheet of red poster board, 14 x 22 inches (36 x 56 cm)
- 1 sheet of white poster board, 14 x 22 inches (36 x 56 cm)
- scissors
- ruler
- 10 iron fishing sinkers, 0.5-ounce (14-gram) each
- 4 stacks of textbooks, each approximately 5 inches (12 cm) tall

Approximate Budget
$15 for poster board and sinkers.

Timetable
Approximately 40 minutes.

How to Work Safely
Use only iron fishing sinkers for weights in this experiment. If only lead sinkers are available, substitute coins or some other easily measurable form of weights. Lead is toxic and should not be handled without proper protection.

OPPOSITE PAGE:
This modern-day bridge combines the arch and the beam designs.

Step-by-Step Instructions

1. Cut two pieces of white poster board, 14 x 4 inches (36 x 10 centimeters). These will be the platforms of your bridges.

2. Cut two pieces of red poster board, 14 x 5 inches (36 x 12 centimeters). These will be the support designs (beam and arch) of your bridges.

TOP: Steps 4 and 6:
Set-up of arch bridge.

BOTTOM: Steps 5 and 6:
Set-up of beam bridge.

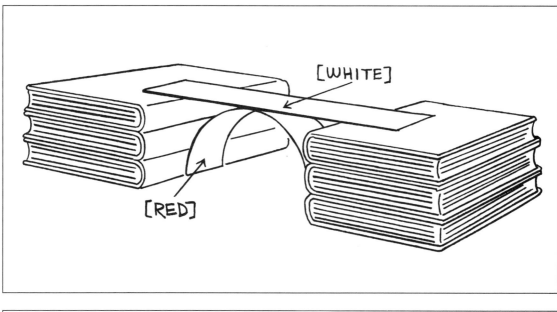

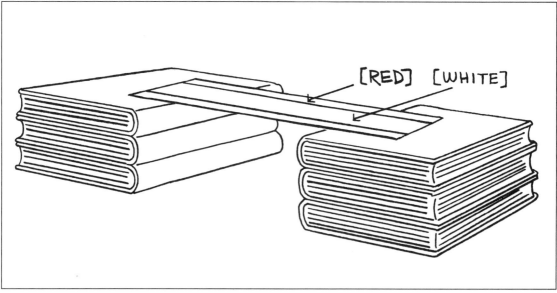

experiment
CENTRAL

3. Place two stacks of textbooks about 8 inches (20 centimeters) apart. Do the same with the other two stacks. These will be the vertical supports of your bridges.

4. Bend one piece of red poster board into an arch and place it between one pair of vertical supports. This will be the arch of one bridge. The peak of the arch should be the same height as the vertical supports. Adjust the distance between the vertical supports until the peak of the arch is even with the top of the two stacks.

5. Lay the other red piece across the second pair of vertical supports. This will be the beam of the other bridge. Adjust the distance between the vertical supports until it is the same as the distance on the arch bridge.

6. Measure and mark the centers of the two pieces of white poster board. Lay each of the white pieces across a pair of vertical supports so that the center mark is halfway across the opening. These will be the platforms of your bridges. The weights must be placed on or near the centerpoints you marked on the platforms. Your bridges should look like the illustrations on page 638.

7. Measure the height of the platforms (at the center) and record this height on a data chart. Place one weight on the center point of each bridge. Measure any distance the center of the platform has dropped. Record this on your data chart. Add another weight as close to the first as possible and measure the height again.

8. Continue adding weights to the bridges. Measure and record the distance each platform drops after each new weight is added. Repeat this process until both of the bridges have collapsed.

Summary of Results

Examine your data and compare the results of the tests for the two designs. Did your predictions prove true? Which design proved to be the sturdier one? Summarize your results in writing.

Change the Project

By altering the project, you can investigate other questions about bridges. How does doubling the thickness of the arch or the beam affect its strength? What if you construct the arch bridge with two

experiment
CENTRAL

Structures and Shapes • 639

Troubleshooter's Guide

Here is a problem you may encounter during this project, some possible causes, and ways to solve the problem.

Problem: One of the bridges tends to twist and dump its weight before collapsing.

Possible causes:

1. Your weights are off center. Place your weights as close to the center mark as possible.

2. Your poster board is not rigid enough. Use thicker poster board.

arches instead of one? Also consider changing the materials. Is rigidity always a good thing? See which supports more weight, a slightly flexible design made of cardboard, or an identical design made of wooden hobby sticks.

Project 2

Beams and Rigidity: How does the vertical height of a beam affect its rigidity?

Purpose

Rigidity is a measure of how much an object, such as a bridge, will deflect when supporting a weight. Bridges must not only be strong, but they must also be fairly rigid to keep the platform level without sagging. In this project, you will construct three beam-support bridges using beams of different vertical heights. You will test each one and compare the results to determine whether increasing the height of a beam can make this bridge design more rigid.

Level of Difficulty

Moderate.

Materials Needed

- 1 sheet of red poster board, 14 x 27 inches (36 x 68 centimeters) or the equivalent with 2 sheets.

- 1 sheet of white poster board, 14 x 22 inches (36 x 56 centimeters)
- scissors
- tape
- ruler
- 10 iron fishing sinkers, 0.5-ounce (14-gram) each
- 6 stacks of textbooks, each approximately 5 inches (12 centimeters) tall

Approximate Budget
$15 for poster board and sinkers.

Timetable
Approximately 40 minutes.

Step-by-Step Instructions
1. Cut three pieces of white poster board, all 14 x 4 inches (36 x 10 centimeters). These will be the platforms of your bridges.

2. Cut three pieces of red poster board, 14 x 6 inches (36 x 15 centimeters), 14 x 9 inches (36 x 23 centimeters), and 14 x 12 inches (36 x 30 centimeters). These will be used to make the beams of your bridges.

3. Place the stacks of textbooks in three pairs. The stacks should be about 10 inches (25 centimeters) apart. These will be the vertical supports of your bridges.

4. On the 14 x 6-inch piece of red poster board, measure and mark the board so the 6-inch (15-centimeter) width is divided into six 1-inch (2.5-centimeter) segments. Fold the board carefully along these marks so it looks like the illustration on page 642.

How to Work Safely
Use only iron fishing sinkers for weights in this experiment. If only lead sinkers are available, substitute coins or some other easily measurable form of weights. Lead is toxic and should not be handled without proper protection.

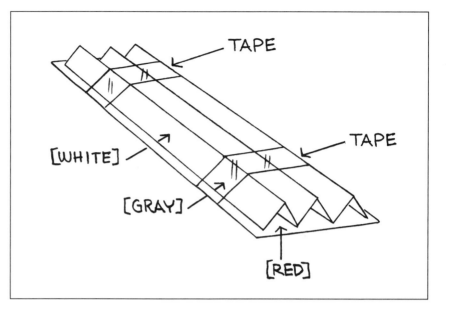

Step 4: Illustration of accordion-fold beam.

5. Divide the 14 x 9-inch poster board into six 1.5-inch- (3.8 centimeter-) wide segments and divide the 14 x 12-inch poster board into six 2-inch- (5 centimeter-) wide segments. Carefully fold each one into an accordion shape.

6. Lay the three folded red pieces across the three pairs of vertical supports. These will be the beams of the bridges.

7. Measure and mark the centers of the three pieces of white poster board. These will be the platforms of your bridges. The weights must be placed on or near the centerpoints you marked on the platforms.

8. Attach the platforms to the beams using tape. Place the beam/platform assemblies across the three pairs of vertical supports with the beam-side down. Your bridges should look like the illustration.

9. Measure the vertical height of each bridge, from the bottom of the folded beam to the top of the platform. Record this information on a data chart.

10. Measure the height of the platforms at the center and record this height on your data chart. Place one weight on the center point of each bridge. Measure the distance the center of the platform has dropped. Record this on your data chart. Add another weight as close to the first as possible and measure again.

experiment
CENTRAL

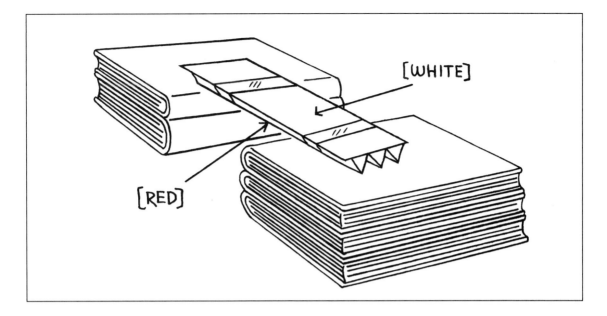

[WHITE]

[RED]

11. Continue adding weight to the bridges. Measure and record the distance each platform drops after each new weight is added. Repeat this process until both of the bridges have collapsed.

Steps 6 to 8: Set-up of beam bridge.

Summary of Results

Examine your data and compare the results of the tests for the three beams. Did your predictions prove true? How much does each increase

Troubleshooter's Guide

Here is a problem you may encounter, some possible causes, and ways to solve the problem.

Problem: The accordion folds of the beams tend to flatten out, decreasing the vertical height of the beam.

Possible causes:

1. Your tape is not holding. Try folding the edges of the white platform around the beam and then taping the assembly.

2. Your poster board is not rigid enough. Use thicker poster board.

in vertical beam height increase the beam's ability to support weight? Summarize your findings in writing.

Change the Project

By altering the project, you can determine whether it is preferable to construct a wide bridge with a low vertical height or a narrow bridge with a greater vertical height. Which is stronger, a bridge 4 feet (1.2 meter) wide and 2 feet (0.6 meter) high, or a bridge 2 feet (0.6 meter) wide and 4 feet (1.2 meter) high? Also consider changing the materials. Is rigidity always a good thing? See which supports more weight, a slightly flexible design made of cardboard or an identical design made of wooden hobby sticks.

 **Design Your Own Experiment**

How to Select a Topic Relating to this Concept

Watching the way your bridge designs reacted to the weight placed on them may have already given you ideas for improving them. Architecture and design engineering encompasses a wide range of structures and products you see and use every day. Can you think of a way to make something work better or keep people safer? Testing ideas in miniature is a vital tool for trying out new ideas.

Think about combining the ideas and designs used in these projects. Can you think of a way to use the strongest beams in the second project to make a stronger arch? Can you build a bridge that uses both a beam and an arch? If you are doing a project as a group, try holding a competition for bridge designs.

If you want to do an experiment or a project, check the For More Information section and talk with your science teacher or school or community media specialist to start gathering information on structure and shape questions that interest you.. As you consider possible experiments or projects, be sure to discuss them with your science teacher or another knowledgeable adult before trying them. Some of them might be dangerous.

Steps in the Scientific Method

To do an original experiment, you need to plan carefully and think things through. Otherwise, you might not be sure which question you are answering, what you are or should be measuring, and what your findings prove or disprove.

Here are the steps in designing an experiment:

- State the purpose of—and the underlying question behind—the experiment you propose to do.
- Recognize the variables involved and select one that will help you answer the question at hand.
- State your hypothesis, an educated guess about the answer to your question.
- Decide how to change the variable you have selected.
- Decide how to measure your results.

Recording Data and Summarizing the Results

In the projects included here and in any experiments or projects you develop, you can look for ways to display your data in more accurate and interesting ways. For example, can you think of a better way to measure the weight sustained by the bridge? Should you test the structures by distributing the weight across the span?

Remember that those who view your results may not have seen the experiment performed, so you must present the information you have gathered in as clear a way as possible. Including photographs or illustrations of the steps in the experiment is a good way to show a viewer how you got from your hypothesis to your conclusion.

Related Projects

To develop other experiments or projects on this topic, take a look at the structures and shapes of things you see around you every day. Take different design options and test them in miniature. Consider ways you could reinforce the bridges you built to enable them to hold more weight. Can you think of a better way to construct new models?

For More Information

Gibson, Gary. *Making Shapes.* Brookfield, CT: Copper Beech Books, 1995. ❖ Demonstrates a variety of structural shapes and how they are applied in construction.

Hawkes, Nigel. *Structures: The Way Things are Built.* New York: MacMillan Publishing Company, 1990. ❖ Looks at ancient and modern structures and describes how they were built.

Stevenson, Neil. *Architecture: The World's Greatest Buildings Explored and Explained.*
New York: DK Publishing, 1997. ❖ Examines in depth the history, design, and construction of fifty buildings and structures from around the world.

The Visual Dictionary of Buildings. New York: DK Publishing, 1992. ❖ Clearly illustrates and provides terminology for numerous architectural features from ancient to modern times.

chapter 43

Tropisms

Why do plants grow toward light? How far will plants stretch to reach light? These questions fascinated the famous British biologist Charles Darwin (1809–1882), who is best known for formulating the theory of natural selection. Also called survival of the fittest, natural selection is the process by which plants and animals best adapted to their environment to survive and pass their traits on to their offspring. Darwin studied **tropism,** which includes the bending of plants toward light, because he believed that this trait helped plants reach the light they needed to survive.

In 1880, Darwin performed experiments showing how the growing tip of a plant bends toward a light source. This behavior is called **phototropism.** *Photo* means "light," and *tropism* means "the growth or movement of a plant toward or away from a stimulus." Thus, *phototropism* means "the tendency of a plant to

Charles Darwin, who helped us understand evolution, also studied plant growth. (Library of Congress)

ⓦWords to Know

Auxins:
Plant hormones that strongly affect plant growth.

Control experiment:
A set-up that is identical to the experiment but is not affected by the variable that affects the experimental group.

grow toward a source of light." At the same time, Darwin noticed that some shade-loving plants turn away from light, a behavior called negative phototropism.

Darwin also discovered another kind of tropism: **geotropism,** meaning "a bending toward Earth." He found that the roots of plants are sensitive to **gravity,** the attraction of Earth's mass on objects, and grow toward the center of gravity, which is the planet's core.

Auxins hold the key

In 1926, Dutch botanist Fritz W. Went discovered that a group of plant hormones called **auxins** strongly affect plant growth. **Hormones** are chemicals produced in the cells of plants and animals that control bodily functions. Stem cells with a large supply of auxins grow faster than stem cells with just a little of these hormones. Auxins are repelled (turned away) by sunlight, so when light shines on one side of a stem, the auxin moves toward the shady side. Thus, growth slows or stops on the side facing the light. While the shady side of the stem grows more quickly, the sunny side remains nearly the same. In time, the longer side of the stem arcs over the shorter side, bending the plant toward the light.

Roots' reaction to gravity is also controlled by the hormone auxin. However, although auxin speeds the growth of cells in plant stems, it

LEFT: Auxins have caused the shady side of the plant stems to grow more quickly than the sunny side, turning the plant toward the light. (Photo Researchers Inc. Reproduced by permission.)

RIGHT: Auxins cause roots to grow longer on their top side, pushing the root toward the ground.

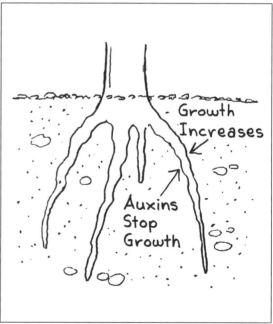

slows the growth of cells in roots. For example, if a plant in a pot is turned on its side, gravity pulls the auxin to the underside of the root, where it slows growth. Then the top side of the root grows more quickly. As the top side grows longer than the underside, the root is forced downward toward Earth. This behavior makes sure that the roots grow deep into the soil, anchoring the plant. At the same time, the stem of the plant grows away from gravity, a negative geotropism. This behavior exposes the leaves to sunlight, which the plant needs for **photosynthesis.**

Reaching out—to water and fence posts

Two growing behaviors do not seem to be controlled by auxins. A behavior called **hydrotropism** causes roots to grow toward a water source. This behavior is controlled by cells in the growing areas of the roots that are sensitive to the presence of water. The root cells grow at different rates, bending the root in the direction of the water. Growing toward water increases the plant's chances of survival.

The second behavior occurs in vines and climbing plants and is called **thigmotropism.** *Thigmo-* means "touch"; thigmotropism is the tendency for a plant to grow toward a surface it touches. Vines and climbing plants have delicate stems called tendrils. When a tendril touches a solid object, such as a fence post, plant cells on the side away from the post grow very quickly, pushing the tendril toward the post and making it curl around it. That is how plants such as sweet peas, beans, and morning glories climb fences.

Why are scientists interested in tropisms? Researchers have created chemical growth substances based on auxins that offer many benefits. These artificial auxins can be sprayed or dusted on stored potatoes to slow the growth of

Words to Know

Food webs:
Interconnected sets of food chains, which are a sequence of organisms directly dependent on one another for food.

Geotropism:
The tendency of roots to bend toward Earth.

Gravity:
The attraction of Earth's mass on objects.

Hormones:
Chemicals produced in the cells of plants and animals that control bodily functions.

Hydrotropism:
The tendency of roots to grow toward a water source.

Thigmotropism is the behavior that causes this green bean vine to grow up and around the wire support. (Photo Researchers Inc. Reproduced by permission.)

eyes or on fruit and flower petals to stop them from falling too soon. They can also be used as herbicides to kill broad-leaved weeds. In addition, these "fake" auxins encourage root growth in plant cuttings.

Food webs, interconnected sets of food chains, depend on plants. People are part of food webs, so the world's population also depends on plants. For this reason, we need to learn as much as possible about plant growth to feed our expanding population. Your own experiments can interest and educate others about this vital topic.

Experiment 1
Phototropism: Will plants follow a maze to reach light?

Purpose/Hypothesis
In this experiment, you will find out whether plants will grow sideways through a maze to reach light. Before you begin, make an educated guess about the outcome of this experiment based on your knowledge of plant growth. This educated guess, or prediction, is your **hypothesis.** A hypothesis should explain these things:

- the topic of the experiment
- the variable you will change
- the variable you will measure
- what you expect to happen

A hypothesis must be brief, specific, and measurable. It must be something you can test through observation. Your experiment will prove or disprove whether your hypothesis is correct. Here is one possible hypothesis for this experiment: "A plant will grow sideways through a maze to reach a light that is about 10 inches (25 centimeters) away."

In this case, the **variable** you will change is the position of the light, and the variable you will measure is the plant's growth toward the light. You expect the plant to grow sideways through the maze toward the light positioned at the other end of the maze.

Setting up a **control experiment** will help you isolate one variable. Only one variable will change between the control plant, which is not being "experimented on," and the experimental plant. That variable is the position of the light. The light will continue to be overhead for the

What Are the Variables?

Variables are anything that might affect the results of an experiment. The main variables in this experiment are:

- the type and health of the plants
- the position and strength of the light
- the distance from the plant to the light
- the temperature where the plants are placed
- the amount of water they receive

In other words, the variables in this experiment are everything that might affect plant growth. If you change more than one variable during the experiment, you will not be able to tell which variable had the most effect on plant growth.

control plant, as usual. It will be coming from the side for the experimental plant.

You will measure the direction of growth for the experimental plant and the control plant. If the experimental plant grows sideways while the control plant continues to grow upright, you will know your hypothesis is correct.

Level of Difficulty

Moderate, because of the time involved.

Materials Needed

- 2 small potatoes with eyes (buds)
- 2 small planting pots with saucers
- potting soil
- scissors
- an empty shoe box with a top
- 3 strips of cardboard, each about 5 inches (12.5 centimeters) long and as wide as the height of the shoe box
- masking tape
- ruler
- water
- a warm, sunny spot

Approximate Budget

$2 for the potatoes and planting materials.

Timetable

1 to 2 weeks for the potato plants to sprout; plus 1 to 2 weeks for the experiment once the plants have sprouted.

Step-by-Step Instructions

1. Allow the potatoes to sit in a warm, sunny place for a week or two until their buds (eyes) start to grow.

2. Plant each potato in a pot with the eye or eyes just above soil level. Water both pots.

3. Take the cover off the shoe box. Cut a section about 2 inches (5 centimeters) square out of one end. (See illustration on page 653.)

4. Follow these steps to form a maze inside the box:

   a. Tape one cardboard strip to the right side and bottom of the box about 2 inches (5 centimeters) from end. (It should end about 2 inches [5 centimeters] from the left side of the box.)

   b. Tape another strip to the left side and bottom of the box about 2 inches (5 centimeters) from the first strip. (It should end about 2 inches [5 centimeters] from the right side of the box.)

   c. Repeat for the third strip, taping it to the right side and bottom of the box, as shown in illustration.

   d. Leave space at the far end of the box for a potato plant.

5. Place one potato plant in the far end of the box. This is your experimental plant. Place the other potato plant outside of—but near—

How to Experiment Safely

Use caution when handling hot lamps. Be sure the lamps and light bulbs are not touching the boxes or plants. Turn off the lights and move the lamps aside before watering the plants to avoid a possible electrical shock.

the box, where it will get the same amount of sun as the box. This second plant is your control experiment.

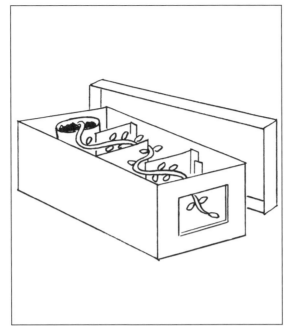

Steps 3 to 5: Set-up of shoe box maze.

6. Water both plants, if needed, and put the lid on the shoe box.

7. Every day, take the lid off the shoe box. Use the ruler to measure the growth and direction of growth of both plants. Record this information on a chart (see illustration on page 655). Also make sketches of the growth. Keep the lid on the box the rest of the time. Water both plants whenever the soil feels dry.

Summary of Results

Create a chart like the one shown to record your findings. Be sure to record your observations every day. Make the chart easy to read, as it will become part of your display.

After the plant has been growing in the box for a week or two, study your chart and sketches and decide whether your hypothesis is correct. Did the experimental plant grow through the maze to reach the light? Did the control plant grow upward toward the light, as plants usually do? Write a paragraph summarizing your findings and explaining whether your hypothesis was correct and how you know.

Change the Variables

You can vary this experiment by changing the variables. For example, use rooted avocado pits or sunflower or bean seedlings. Just make sure the experimental and control plants are identical and healthy. You can also move the position of the light. Construct identical mazes in two shoe boxes. Then place one box flat, as in this experiment, and one on end with the light hole at the top. Put a plant at the far end of the first box

Troubleshooter's Guide

Experiments do not always work out as planned. However, figuring out what went wrong can definitely be a learning experience. Here are some problems that may arise during this experiment, some possible causes, and ways to remedy the problems.

Problem: One or both plants are not growing at all.

Possible cause: The plant may have been diseased or infested with insects. Dispose of both plants in case they are both diseased, and repeat the experiment with different plants.

Problem: The control plant is growing sideways, too.

Possible cause: The light might have been coming from a low position, perhaps blocked by a window blind. Remove any obstructions and make sure the light comes from overhead. The control plant should begin growing upright.

Problem: The experimental plant is growing straight up and pushing against the top of the box.

Possible causes:

1. Light might have been seeping in through cracks in the box, drawing the plant upward. Cover the box with a towel, making sure not to cover the light hole at the end. Also, make sure to replace the box lid immediately after making your daily growth measurements.

2. The light source might not have been strong enough to reach the plant at the far end of the box. Place both plants in a sunnier spot or remove one cardboard strip to let in more light.

Problem: By the end of a week, the experimental plant has barely started to grow through the maze.

Possible causes: You might not have allowed enough time, or the plant may be growing slowly because of cool temperatures or too little light. If you remedy these problems, the plant should continue to grow or grow faster.

experiment
CENTRAL

		Sun.	Mon.	Tues.	Wed.	Thurs.	Fri.	Sat.
Experiment plant	Growth in cm.							
	Sketch							
Control plant	Growth in cm.							
	Sketch							

and at the bottom of the second box. See whether plants move faster through the maze when they are growing up or growing sideways. Finally, you can change the distance of the light from the plants. Construct more elaborate mazes to test the limits of a plant's efforts to reach the light.

Step 7: Recording chart for Experiment 1.

Experiment 2
Geotropism: Will plant roots turn toward the pull of gravity?

Purpose/Hypothesis
In this experiment, you will find out whether plant roots change the direction they are growing as their position is changed in relation to the pull of gravity. Before you begin, make an educated guess about the outcome of this experiment based on your knowledge of plant growth.

This educated guess, or prediction, is your **hypothesis.** A hypothesis should explain these things:

- the topic of the experiment
- the variable you will change
- the variable you will measure
- what you expect to happen

A hypothesis must be brief, specific, and measurable. It must be something you can test through observation. Your experiment will prove or disprove whether your hypothesis is correct. Here is one possible hypothesis for this experiment: "Roots will change the direction they grow as their position is changed in relation to the pull of gravity."

In this case, the **variable** you will change is the direction of the pull of gravity, and the variable you will measure is the direction of root growth. You expect the roots to grow toward the pull of gravity.

Setting up a **control experiment** will help you isolate one variable. Only one variable will change between the control seeds, which are not being "experimented on," and the experimental seeds. That variable is the direction of the pull of gravity, the attraction of Earth's mass on objects. Gravity will continue to pull from the bottom for the control seeds as they remain with their roots pointing down. Gravity will seem to pull from different directions as you turn the experimental seeds so their roots point in various directions.

 What Are the Variables?

Variables are anything that might affect the results of an experiment. Here are the main variables in this experiment:

- the type of seeds and their germination rate
- the amount of light and water the seeds receive
- the temperature where the seeds are placed
- the direction of the pull of gravity

In other words, the variables in this experiment are everything that might affect the direction of root growth. If you change more than one variable during the experiment, you will not be able to tell which variable had the most effect on the roots.

You will record the direction of root growth for the experimental seeds and the control seeds. If the roots of the experimental seeds grow in different directions as you turn them, while the control seeds' roots continue to grow straight down, you will know your hypothesis is correct. The experimental roots will be turning toward the direction of the pull of gravity.

Level of Difficulty

Moderate, because of the time involved.

Materials Needed

You can complete this experiment using small panes of glass held together with rubber bands and set in cake pans. As an alternative, you can use large glass jars with lids. The panes are easier to turn to encourage roots to grow in a circle. However, glass panes are more expensive and require careful handling to avoid accidents.

- four 10-inch (25-centimeter) squares of glass with the edges taped for safety
- 8 large rubber bands
- 2 cake pans or other flat containers, large enough to hold the squares of glass standing on an edge
- bean or sunflower seeds
- paper towels
- water
- eyedropper
- warm, sunny spot
- optional: camera and film

Approximate Budget

$16 for four 10-inch (25-centimeter) squares of double-strength glass (or $8 for the same amount of single-strength glass); about $1 for seeds.

Timetable

2 to 3 weeks for the roots to complete a circle.

Step-by-Step Instructions

1. Cut 5 or 6 layers of paper towels to form a 10-inch (25-centimeter) square pad.

2. Place the pad on one glass square and cover the pad with enough water to moisten it.

How to Experiment Safely

The edges of glass panes can be razor sharp. Ask an adult to wrap all edges of the glass with tape to prevent cuts. Then be careful in handling the glass so it does not break.

3. Arrange 6 to 8 seeds in a circle on the pad.

4. Carefully place another square of glass on top, so the pad and seeds are like the filling in a sandwich.

5. Place 4 rubber bands around the "sandwich," at the top, bottom, and both sides, to hold it together.

    Alternative method: Fill a jar with damp, crumpled paper towels. Then carefully place the seeds in a row around the inside of the jar between the towels and the glass.

LEFT: Steps 4 to 7: Set-up of control and experimental glass pane "sandwiches."

RIGHT: Step 10: Experimental "sandwich" with roots formed into a circle.

6. Repeat steps 1 through 5 to create a control experiment.

7. Place the cake pans side by side in a warm, sunny spot. Stand each

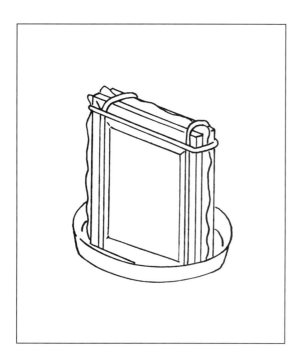

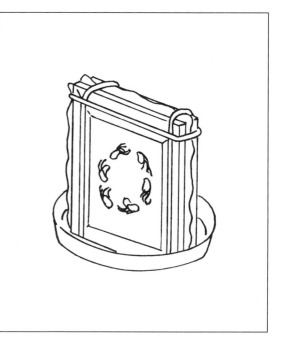

"sandwich" vertically in a cake pan, propping it up with books or other supports, if necessary. If you are using the alternative method, place the jars side by side in a warm, sunny spot.

8. Leave the control sandwich (or control jar) in this position throughout the experiment.

9. Use the eyedropper to moisten the towels if they dry out.

10. After the roots have grown about 1 inch (2.5 centimeters), turn the experimental sandwich (or jar) once, resting it on its side. Now the roots should point to the side. In a few days, the roots should bend downward toward the pull of gravity again. Then turn the sandwich once again, so the top is the bottom. When the roots point down again, turn the sandwich again. Continue until the roots form a circle.

Step 11: Recording chart for Experiment 2.

	Sun.	Mon.	Tues.	Wed.	Thurs.	Fri.	Sat.
Experiment seeds							
Control seeds							

11. Every day, record the root growth you see in both experimental and control seeds on a chart (see illustration on page 659). If possible, take photographs of the two sandwiches (or jars) together each time you turn the experimental one.

Troubleshooter's Guide

Experiments do not always work out as planned. However, figuring out what went wrong can definitely be a learning experience. Here are some problems that may arise during this experiment, some possible causes, and ways to remedy the problems.

Problem: One or both sets of seeds did not sprout and/or grow roots.

Possible causes:

1. The seeds may have been diseased or exposed to freezing temperatures or other adverse conditions. Dispose of them, clean the glass panes or jars thoroughly, and repeat the experiment with different seeds.

2. The seeds might have dried out or they might be too cold. Try adding more water or putting the seeds in a warmer spot. Or start again with new seeds.

Problem: The roots of the experimental plant did not form a circle.

Possible cause: They needed more time to grow between turns. Try again, allowing more time.

Problem: The stems of the new plants became tangled in the roots.

Possible cause: As roots grow toward gravity, stems grow away from it. Every time you turned the sandwich or jar, the stem also responded to the change in the pull of gravity. You might try seeds that grow less vigorous plants, such as mustard or radish seeds (which are also smaller and harder to handle). You can point out the stems' response to gravity as part of your experiment as well.

experiment
CENTRAL

Summary of Results

Create a chart like the one illustrated to record your findings. Be sure to record your observations every day. Make the chart easy to read, as it will become part of your display.

Study your chart and decide whether your hypothesis was correct. Did the roots of the experimental seeds change direction as you changed the position of the roots in relation to the pull of gravity? Did the roots of the control seeds continue to grow downward, as they usually do? Write a paragraph summarizing your findings and explaining whether your hypothesis was correct and how your measurements and observations support it.

Change the Variables

There are several ways you can vary this experiment. For example, try different seeds like mustard, radish, or other seeds. You can also change the light. Light one seed sandwich from the top and one from the bottom to see if the position of the light affects how the roots grow. Finally, you can change the amount of water the seeds receive. Set up two seed sandwiches, as in this experiment, then use the eyedropper to water only one section of the paper towels for the experimental seeds. The moisture will spread somewhat, but the farthest, driest roots should turn toward the moisture. This demonstrates **hydrotropism**, growing toward water.

 **Design Your Own Experiment**

How to Select a Topic Relating to this Concept

Whether your interest in plants is old or new, plants offer fascinating questions to explore through science experiments. Consider what puzzles you about plants. What have you wondered about? For example, if you cut the growing tip off a plant, will the remaining stem still turn toward the light? What if you turn a potted plant upside down and put the light source underneath the plant? Will the stem grow downward, toward the light?

Do roots grow differently if the seeds are planted upside down? What happens if you cut the tip off roots? Will they still turn toward the pull of gravity? Which way would roots grow in a zero-gravity environment? How might tropisms affect plants growing in a space station?

Check the For More Information section and talk with your science teacher or school or community media specialist to start gathering information on tropism questions that interest you.

Steps in the Scientific Method

To do an original experiment, you need to plan carefully and think things through. Otherwise, you might not be sure what question you are answering, what you are or should be measuring, or what your findings prove or disprove.

Here are the steps in designing an experiment:

- State the purpose of—and the underlying question behind—the experiment you propose to do.
- Recognize the variables involved, and select one that will help you answer the question at hand.
- State a testable hypothesis, an educated guess about the answer to your question.
- Decide how to change the variable you selected.
- Decide how to measure your results.

Recording Data and Summarizing the Results

In the two tropism experiments, your raw data might include not only charts of measurements of plant or root growth, but also drawings or photographs of these changes.

If you display your experiment, you need to limit the amount of information you offer, so viewers will not be overwhelmed by detail. Make clear your beginning question, the variable you changed, the variable you measured, the results, and your conclusions about plant growth. Viewers—and judges at science fairs—will want to see how each experiment was set up, including the shoe-box maze or seed sandwiches you created. The plants or seeds or a photograph or drawing of the plant or root growth at several stages during the experiment would be valuable and interesting. Be sure to label everything you include clearly to show how it fits together. Viewers will want to know what kinds of plants or seeds you used, how long each step took, and other basic information.

experiment
CENTRAL

Related Projects

There are a variety of projects relating to plants and plant growth that you can undertake. You can make a paper or clay model of the reproductive parts of flowers, or you can collect and display different kinds of plants that have been equally exposed to acid rain. Or you can demonstrate how a process works, such as showing how water circulates through a plant from the roots up the stem and out through the leaves.

For More Information

Alvin, Virginia, and Robert Silverstein. *Plants*. New York: Henry Holt, 1996. ❖ Explains the plant kingdom classifications and specific kinds of plants, from the first seed plants to edible plants.

Capon, Brian. *Plant Survival: Adapting to a Hostile World*. Portland, OR: Timber Press, 1994. ❖ Covers ways that plants have adapted to adverse conditions, such as cold or hot temperature and too much or too little precipitation.

Catherall, Ed. *Exploring Plants*. Austin, TX: Steck-Vaughn, 1992. ❖ Provides information and projects relating to plant structures, functions, reproduction, and growth.

Cochrane, Jennifer. *Nature*. New York: Warwick Press, 1991. ❖ Examines how plants have invaded seemingly inhospitable land and managed to thrive there.

Kerrod, Robin. *Plant Life*. New York: Marshall Cavendish, 1994. ❖ Information about plant biology, groups, and habitats.

Parker, Steve. *Science Project Book of Plants*. New York: Marshall Cavendish, 1989. ❖ Features more experiments and explanations about plants and their growth.

Tesar, Jenny. *Green Plants*. Woodbridge, CT: Blackbirch Press, 1993. ❖ Includes information on the metabolism, reproduction, and growth of plants, plus their reactions to the environment and role in the food web.

Van Cleave, Janice. *Plants: Mind-Boggling Experiments You Can Turn into Science Fair Projects*. New York: Wiley, 1997. ❖ Illustrates possible projects, along with lots of information about plants and plant processes.

chapter 44

Vegetative Propagation

Your grandmother proudly shows you an African violet she has grown from seed. Its flower is really unusual: pink with tiny red dots. She grew this plant by pollinating a pink African violet with a red one and planting the seeds that resulted. You remember that **pollination** is the transfer of pollen from the male reproductive organs to the female reproductive organs of plants. It is a form of **sexual reproduction.**

Only one of your grandmother's seedlings produced dotted flowers. She knows that if she pollinates this special plant with pollen from a different violet, she might not get any more plants with dotted flowers. Pollinated seeds, like the fertilized eggs of animals, contain the characteristics of both parents. The flower-color characteristics of the other violet may be stronger than the ones in the special plant. If so, none of the seedlings from this pollination will have dotted flowers.

Still, your grandmother is smiling. She knows how to grow more of these special plants without using pollen or seeds. She will use vegetative propagation.

What is vegetative propagation?

Vegetative propagation is a form of **asexual reproduction,** a reproductive process that does not involve the union of two individuals in the exchange of genetic material. In sexual reproduction, **genetic material** transfers characteristics from both parents to their offspring. But plants produced by vegetative propagation, or asexual reproduction, have only one parent, so they have the genetic material of only that parent. They are identical to that parent.

ⓦords to Know

Asexual reproduction:
A reproductive process that does not involve the union of two individuals in the exchange of genetic material.

Auxins:
A group of plant hormones responsible for patterns of plant growth.

Carnivore:
A meat-eating organism.

Control experiment:
A setup that is identical to the experiment but is not affected by the variable that will be changed during the experiment.

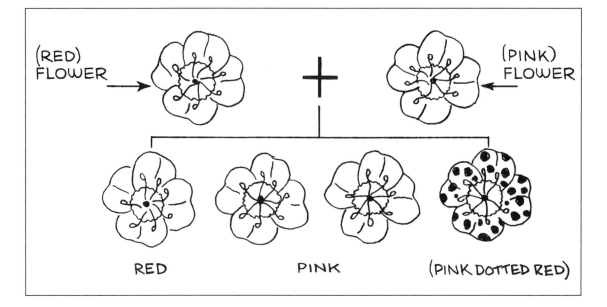

RED FLOWER + PINK FLOWER

RED   PINK   (PINK DOTTED RED)

Pollination mixes the characteristics of two parent plants.

Grandma does not want any new characteristics in her seedlings, just the ones from her special parent plant, so she will grow new violets from that plant's leaf cuttings. Growing plants from leaf cuttings is one form of vegetative propagation. In Experiment 1, you will grow new plants from leaf and stem cuttings.

How can a plant grow from a leaf or stem?

In many plants, cells in the stem tips, root tips, leaves, and certain other areas of the plant are capable of becoming different kinds of plant tissue. These cells allow the stem of a plant to produce roots. They allow the eye, or bud, of a potato to produce both roots that grow downward and shoots that grow upward and become the stems and leaves of a new potato plant. You will explore the growth of potato eyes during Experiment 2.

Plant hormones help control this growth. A **hormone** is a chemical produced in living cells that regulates the functions of the organism. **Auxins** are a group of plant hormones responsible for patterns of plant growth.

When a stem begins to grow horizontally, gravity causes auxin to accumulate on the lower side of the stem. This hormone makes the cells on that side grow longer. This forces the growing tip of the stem to turn upward. Auxin has the opposite effect on roots. A concentra-

Words to Know

Genetic material:
Material that transfers characteristics from a parent to its offspring.

Herbivore:
A plant-eating organism.

Hormone:
A chemical produced in living cells that regulates the functions of the organism.

Humidity:
The amount of water vapor (moisture) contained in the air.

Hypothesis:
An idea in the form of a statement that can be tested by observation and/or experiment.

tion of auxin on the lower side of roots stops growth there. As the top side of the root continues to grow, the root tip turns downward.

English scientist Charles Darwin (1809–1882) noticed that plants' tendency to bend toward light increased the chances of their survival. He figured out that the growing tip of the plant controlled this bending, but it was not until 1926 that the Dutch botanist (one who studies plants) Fritz W. Went isolated the hormone auxin in the growing tip.

Since then, scientists have produced artificial auxins. They are used to improve root growth and produce seedless fruits by stimulating the growth of fruit without pollination. These hormones can also stop fruit from falling from trees before it is ripe. In addition, the hormones slow the ripening of fruit that will be shipped long distances and help preserve potatoes, onions, and other vegetables that will be stored for an extended period. Auxins can also kill weeds by speeding up their growth cycle.

Pollination has produced African violets of many colors in this greenhouse. (Peter Arnold Inc. Reproduced by permission.)

(W)ords to Know

Pollination:
The transfer of pollen from the male reproductive organs to the female reproductive organs of plants.

Auxins can speed up plant growth or slow it down.

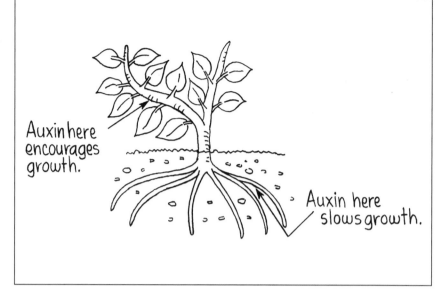

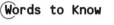

Words to Know

Producer:
An organism that can manufacture its own food from nonliving materials and an external energy source, usually by photosynthesis.

Sexual reproduction:
A reproductive process that involves the union of two individuals in the exchange of genetic material.

Tuber:
An underground, starch-storing stem, such as a potato.

Variable:
Something that can affect the results of an experiment.

Vegetative propagation:
A form of asexual reproduction in which plants are produced that are genetically identical to the parent.

Learning about plant growth can help you increase your plant collection. More importantly, it can enable you to better understand the plants that we depend on for our existence. Without plants, also called **producers,** the plant-eaters or **herbivores** starve. Without herbivores, the meat-eaters or **carnivores** go hungry, too.

 Experiment 1
Auxins: How do auxins affect plant growth?

Purpose/Hypothesis
In this experiment, you will try to produce new plants from stem and leaf cuttings. You will treat half of the cuttings with the plant hormone auxin, while the other half will not be treated. The difference between the two groups of cuttings in root, leaf, and stem growth will tell you whether auxin makes any difference. Before you begin, make an educated guess about the outcome of this experiment based on your knowledge of plant propagation. This educated guess, or prediction, is your **hypothesis.** A hypothesis should explain these things:

*   the topic of the experiment
*   the variable you will change

- the variable you will measure
- what you expect to happen

A hypothesis should be brief, specific, and measurable. It must be something you can test through observation. Your experiment will prove or disprove whether your hypothesis is correct. Here is one possible hypothesis for this experiment: "Stem cuttings treated with auxin will grow more roots, taller stems, and more leaves, and treated leaf cuttings will grow more new plants than will untreated stem and leaf cuttings."

In this case, the variable you will change is the auxin treatment, and the variable you will measure is root, stem, and leaf growth for the stem cuttings and the number of new plants grown by the leaf cuttings. Your untreated cuttings will serve as a **control experiment** to allow you to measure any difference in growth. If the treated cuttings grow more than the untreated ones, you will know your hypothesis is correct.

Whether you are a strict vegetarian or live from hamburger to hamburger, you need plants! (Peter Arnold Inc. Reproduced by permission.)

experiment
CENTRAL

What Are the Variables?

Variables are anything that might affect the results of an experiment. Here are the main variables in this experiment:

- the types and health of the plants from which the cuttings are taken
- the size of the plant cuttings and the locations from which they are taken on the parent plants
- the light, water, soil, and temperature conditions under which the cuttings are grown
- treatment with the hormone auxin

In other words, the variables in this experiment are everything that might affect the growth of the cuttings. If you change more than one variable, you will not be able to tell which variable had the most effect on growth.

Level of Difficulty

Moderate, because of the time and materials involved.

Materials Needed

- stem cuttings from several plants, including geranium, coleus, petunia, fuchsia, dieffenbachia, dracena, philodendron, and ivy
- leaf cuttings from several plants, including African violet, gloxinia, rex begonia, piggyback plant, peperomia, sansevieria, and succulents (such as a jade plant)
- rooting hormone powder, such as Rootone or Hormodin
- pruning shears or scissors
- two 4-inch- (10-centimeter-) diameter pots with saucers for each kind of cutting you plan to make (one pot for the treated cuttings and one for the untreated cuttings)
- potting soil (if possible, mix vermiculite or perlite, two kinds of soil conditioners, into the soil)
- pot labels and a marker
- pencil
- water

- clear plastic bags big enough to fit over each pot
- ruler

Approximate Budget

Costs will depend on whether you need to buy plants or can take cuttings from available plants. Pots cost about $1 each. Potting soil is $3 to $4 for a large bag. A container of Rootone will be $4 to $5.

Timetable

3 weeks for the cuttings to sprout and grow.

Step-by-Step Instructions

1. Label each pair of pots "Experimental" and "Control," along with the name of the plant.

2. Fill each pot with soil, leaving 1 inch or so at the top of pot.

3. Take the cuttings. Make at least two cuttings of each plant for the experimental pot and two identical cuttings of the same plant for the control pot. (You will need extra cuttings in case some die.)

   For stem cuttings from each plant you selected:

   a. Take four 3- to 4-inch (7.5 to 10 centimeter) cuttings from the plant. Slice at an angle to expose as many special growing cells in the stem as possible. Cut just below where a leaf is attached.

   b. Pull off any leaves close to the bottom of the cuttings.

   c. Use the pencil to make two holes 2 inches (5 centimeters) deep in each pot.

   d. Dip about 1 inch (2.5 centimeters) of the end of two cuttings into the container of rooting hormone. Tap the stem to remove excess powder.

How to Experiment Safely

Be very careful in using the shears or scissors to make the cuttings. You might ask an adult to help you. Also try not to get the rooting hormone on your skin or especially in your eyes. Wash your hands after setting up the experiment.

Steps 3d and 3e: Dip cuttings into root hormone and then gently plant them in experimental pot.

e. Gently put the stem of each treated cutting into a hole in the experimental pot without rubbing off the powder. Pat the soil around the cutting.

f. Put the two untreated cuttings into holes in the control pot, and pat the soil around them.

For leaf cuttings from each plant you selected:

g. Cut four healthy leaves from the plant. The leaves might have stems attached or not, but make the cuttings identical.

h. Use the pencil to make two shallow grooves in the potting soil of each pot.

i. Dip the bottom edge (and any stem) of two leaves into the container of rooting hormone. Tap the leaves to remove excess powder.

j. Gently place each treated leaf into the soil in the experimental pot without rubbing off the powder. Pat the soil around it.

k. Put the two untreated leaves into the control pot, and pat the soil around them.

OPPOSITE PAGE:
Step 6: Recording chart for Experiment 1.

4. Water all the cuttings and place the pots in a warm, light spot, but not in direct sunlight.

Record of Growth

Stem Cuttings	End of Week 1	End of Week 2	End of Week 3
Experimental cuttings, (plant name) Beginning height: Beginning number of leaves:	Height: Number of leaves: Other growth:	Height: Number of leaves: Other growth:	Height: Number of leaves: Other growth: Root growth:
Control cuttings, (same plant) Beginning height: Beginning number of leaves:	Height: Number of leaves: Other growth:	Height: Number of leaves: Other growth:	Height: Number of leaves: Other growth: Root growth:

Leaf Cuttings	End of Week 1	End of Week 2	End of Week 3
Experimental cuttings, (plant name)	Growth observed:	Growth observed:	Growth observed: Root growth:
Control cuttings, (same plant)	Growth observed:	Growth observed:	Growth observed: Root growth:

5. Place a plastic bag loosely over each pot to keep the humidity level high around the cuttings. **Humidity** is the amount of water vapor (moisture) contained in the air. The cuttings will all have a better chance of taking root and growing if the air around them is moist.

6. Observe and record any visible growth on a chart similar to the one illustrated on page 673. Stem cuttings may grow taller and grow more leaves. Leaf cuttings may sprout tiny leaves at their base.

7. Check the soil in each pot twice a week and water any pots that feel dry.

8. At the end of Week 3, gently pull each cutting out of its pot, shake off the soil, and record the number and length of any roots that have grown.

Summary of Results

Use the data on your chart to create some or all of these graphs:

- a line graph comparing the height of the experimental and control stem cuttings at the end of each week
- a line or bar graph comparing the leaf growth of the two groups of stem cuttings at the end of each week
- a bar graph comparing the number of new plants growing on the leaf cuttings at the end of each week
- a chart comparing the final root growth of all cuttings, carefully labeling the stem and leaf cuttings

Then study the graphs and your growth chart and decide whether your hypothesis was correct. Did the experimental stem cuttings show more stem, leaf, and root growth than the control cuttings? Did the experimental leaf cuttings grow more tiny new plants than the control cuttings? Write a paragraph summarizing your findings and explaining whether they support your hypothesis.

Change the Variables

Here are some ways to vary this experiment:

- Use cuttings from plants that are harder to root, such as woody stem cuttings from a rose bush.
- Try a variation on leaf cuttings: cut rex begonia leaves into wedge-shaped pieces or cut sansevieria leaves horizontally into short

Troubleshooter's Guide

Here are some problems that may arise during this experiment, some possible causes, and ways to remedy the problems.

Problem: All or most of the cuttings rotted.

Possible cause: The humidity was too high. Try again, watering the cuttings less or not using the plastic bags.

Problem: All or most of the cuttings dried up.

Possible causes:

1. The cuttings needed more water. Try again, checking every other day to see if the soil has dried out.

2. The cuttings received too much direct sun. Place them where they will receive light but not direct sun.

Problem: The control cuttings from one kind of plant grew more than the experimental cuttings from another kind of plant.

Possible cause: Different types of plants have different growth rates. Focus on whether cuttings from the same plant grew better when they were treated with the rooting hormone.

lengths. Dip the bottom edges of some pieces into rooting hormone, and plant in potting soil.

- Treat all cuttings with rooting hormone and experiment with the amount of humidity around the cuttings to see how that affects their growth.
- Root the cuttings in water instead of soil. Cover the top of the water containers with clear plastic wrap or aluminum foil and make a hole for each cutting. Stir rooting hormone into the water of some cuttings to see if it improves root growth under these conditions.
- Sprinkle seeds with rooting hormone before planting them. Compare their growth with that of untreated seeds.

Experiment 2
Potatoes from Pieces: How do potatoes reproduce vegetatively?

Purpose/Hypothesis

In this experiment, you will cut up potatoes and plant different parts of them to determine which parts can be used for vegetative propagation. The potatoes we eat are actually **tubers,** which are underground, starch-storing stems. The eyes, or buds, on one potato can develop into several identical new plants through vegetative propagation. The starch stored in the potato or tuber provides food for the new plant until it develops its own root system.

Here are the questions to investigate: Do only the eyes of potatoes develop into new plants? What about chunks of potato without eyes? And will eyes grow without any potato attached? To find out, you will plant some chunks of potato with eyes, some chunks without eyes, and some eyes without potatoes attached.

Before you begin, make an educated guess about the outcome of this experiment based on your knowledge of plant propagation. This educated guess, or prediction, is your **hypothesis.** A hypothesis should explain these things:

- the topic of the experiment
- the variable you will change
- the variable you will measure
- what you expect to happen

A hypothesis should be brief, specific, and measurable. It must be something you can test through observation. Your experiment will prove or disprove whether your hypothesis is correct. Here is one possible hypothesis for this experiment: "Only chunks of potatoes with eyes will develop into new potato plants."

In this case, the **variable** you will change is whether the potato has an eye, and the variable you will measure is the presence or absence of new growth. Your **control experiment** will consist of planting potato chunks without eyes and planting eyes without potato chunks attached to them. If only the chunks with eyes sprout, you will know that your hypothesis is correct. This result will prove that the special cells in plant stems and leaves that can develop into different kinds of plant

experiment
CENTRAL

What Are the Variables?

Variables are anything that might affect the results of an experiment. Here are the main variables in this experiment:

- the kind of potatoes used

- the light, water, soil, and temperature conditions under which the potato parts are grown

- the presence of eyes in the potato chunks

- whether the eyes have potato attached

In other words, the variables in this experiment are everything that might affect the growth of new potato plants. If you change more than one variable, you will not be able to tell which variable had the most effect on the new plant growth.

tissue are also present in potato eyes. However, the eyes require the starch food in potatoes in order to reproduce successfully.

Level of Difficulty

Moderate, because of the time involved.

Materials Needed

- 2 or 3 seed potatoes (available at garden supply stores or farmers' markets) or other potatoes that have not been treated to stop the growth of eyes
- three 5- or 6-inch- (12- or 15-centimeter-) diameter pots and saucers
- pot labels and a marker
- potting soil (if possible, mix vermiculite or perlite into the soil)
- sharp knife and cutting board
- water
- ruler

Approximate Budget

$6 for potatoes, pots, and potting soil.

Timetable

3 weeks.

How to Experiment Safely

Take care in cutting the potatoes into chunks. You might ask an adult to help you.

Step-by-Step Instructions

1. Locate the green or white eyes on the potatoes. If there are no eyes yet, place the potatoes in a shallow dish that contains about 1 inch (2.5 centimeters) of water. Leave the dish in a sunny place for several days, and eyes should appear.

2. Carefully cut up the potatoes, creating two or three chunks with eyes attached. Also create two or three chunks that do not have eyes. One surface of these chunks should be covered with potato skin.

3. Use your fingernail to gently separate two or three eyes from a potato.

4. Mark the three pots *Chunks with eyes, Chunks without eyes,* and *Eyes only.*

Steps 4 and 5: Set-up of three pots with soil and potato chunks.

5. Fill each pot about half full of soil and place the appropriate chunks or eyes on the soil. Cover with more soil.

experiment
CENTRAL

Growth Record

	End of Week 1	End of Week 2	End of Week 3
Potato chunks without eyes	Growth observed:	Growth observed:	Growth observed:
Potato chunks without eyes	Growth observed:	Growth observed:	Growth observed:
Eyes with no potato attached	Growth observed:	Growth observed:	Growth observed:

6. Water all pots and place them in a warm, sunny location.

7. Observe and record any growth you see, using a chart like the one illustrated. Feel the soil every other day and add water when it seems dry.

Step 7: Recording chart for Experiment 2.

Summary of Results

Study the findings on your chart and decide whether your hypothesis was correct. Did only the potato chunks with eyes sprout? Did the eyes without potato attached sprout and then die? Write a paragraph summarizing your findings and explaining whether they support your hypothesis.

Change the Variables

Here are ways to vary this experiment:

- Use a different type of potato, such as baking, red, or sweet potatoes, to see if the experiment results change.
- Leave different amounts of potato attached to the eyes to determine how much potato results in the best growth.

Troubleshooter's Guide

Here are some problems that may arise during this experiment, some possible causes, and ways to remedy the problems.

Problem: Nothing in any of the pots sprouted.

Possible causes:

1. The pots might have been too cold or the soil too dry. Try again, providing good growing conditions for all the pots.

2. The potatoes might have been old or diseased. Try again with new potatoes.

Problem: Some of the chunks without eyes sprouted.

Possible cause: Perhaps they contained eyes that had not yet broken through the potato's skin. Take the chunks out of the soil and see if eyes have developed. If so, eliminate them from your experiment.

Problem: Some of the eyes without potato attached are growing.

Possible cause: A small amount of potato might be attached, providing a temporary source of food. Continue the experiment to see if the eyes keep growing. (They might, if they develop roots quickly enough.)

- Sprinkle a rooting hormone on potato chunks, with and without eyes, to see if it changes the results of the experiment. (Versions of the growth hormone auxin are often sprayed on potatoes to slow the growth of eyes. Auxin can both promote and discourage plant growth, depending on how much is used and when it is applied.)

Design Your Own Experiment

How to Select a Topic Relating to this Concept

You can explore many other aspects of vegetative propagation. Consider what you would like to know about this topic. For example, you might investigate growing new plants by using runners (strawberries and spider plants), suckers (succulents such as aloe), or air-layering (dieffenbachia and dracena).

Check the For More Information section and talk with your science teacher or school or community media specialist to start gathering information on plant growth questions that interest you. As you consider possible experiments, be sure to discuss them with your science teacher or another knowledgeable adult before trying them. Some of the chemicals or procedures might be dangerous.

Steps in the Scientific Method

To do an original experiment, you need to plan carefully and think things through. Otherwise, you might not be sure which question you are answering, what you are or should be measuring, or what your findings prove or disprove.

Here are the steps in designing an experiment:

- State the purpose of—and the underlying question behind—the experiment you propose to do.
- Recognize the variables involved, and select one that will help you answer the question.
- State a testable hypothesis, an educated guess about the answer to your question.
- Decide how to change the variable you selected.
- Decide how to measure your results.

Recording Data and Summarizing the Results

In the plant growth experiments, your raw data might include charts, graphs, drawings, and photographs of the changes you observed. If you display your experiment, make clear the question you were answering, the variable you changed, the variable you measured, the results, and your conclusions. Explain what materials you used, how long each step took, and other basic information.

Related Projects

You can undertake a variety of projects related to vegetative propagation. For example, how small a piece of a leaf will produce new plants? Will all parts of a leaf produce new plants equally well? Will a bulb (an underground stem, like a potato) produce two identical plants if it is cut in half and both parts are planted? Which will bloom first, a plant grown from seed or a plant reproduced vegetatively?

For More Information

Alvin, Virginia, and Robert Silverstein. *Plants*. New York: Twenty-First Century Books, 1996. ❖ Offers a general description of the plant kingdom and its classification system, along with discussion of specific kinds of plants, such as poisonous ones.

Bleifeld, Maurice. *Botany Projects for Young Scientists*. New York: Franklin Watts, 1992. ❖ Contains a collection of activities and experiments, exploring photosynthesis, plant structures, and growth.

Bochinski, Julianne Blair. *The Complete Handbook of Science Fair Projects*. New York: Wiley, 1991. ❖ Offers guidance in choosing and completing science fair projects, including several dealing with plants and plant growth.

Hershey, David. *Plant Biology Science Projects*. New York: Wiley, 1995. ❖ Outlines plant-related science projects that will interest young adults.

Kenda, Margaret, and Phyllis W. Williams. *Science Wizardry for Kids*. New York: Barron's, 1992. ❖ Describes how to complete basic experiments on topics such as plants, animals, sound, light, and the weather.

Van Cleave, Janice. *Spectacular Science Projects with Plants*. New York: Wiley, 1997. ❖ Presents facts and experiments relating to plants.

experiment
CENTRAL

chapter 45

Volcanoes

On August 24, in 79 A.D., the citizens of Pompeii, in what is now Italy, woke up to a warm, sunny day. Some probably went to sit outside their beautiful villas to sit and admire the fruit trees, ornamental wall paintings, and statues in their enclosed gardens. Many of the villas overlooked the sparkling Bay of Naples. Businesses were opening and some were already bustling with activity. But life in Pompeii ended abruptly that morning when nearby Mount Vesuvius erupted. Pompeii and the neighboring town of Herculaneum were destroyed. More than 2,000 people were suffocated by the gas and ash that spewed from Vesuvius and covered Pompeii or by the **lava** flow of molten rock that leveled Herculaneum. Pliny the Younger, a Roman historian, saw the terrible event from the nearby town of Miseneum and wrote the first written, eyewitness account of a volcano's eruption.

Today Vesuvius is still an active **volcano,** a conical or domelike mountain of lava, ash, and cinders that forms around a vent leading to molten rock deep within Earth. When volcanoes erupt, they literally blow their top, ejecting tons of rock and debris into the air, as well as sending clouds of toxic gases and steam and rivers of lava down the sides of the mountain.

Get the drift?

After the Americas were discovered, scientists observed that Earth's continents fit together like the pieces of a jigsaw puzzle. The scientists believed that the continents had once been joined together in one land mass and then violently separated. In 1912, German meteorologist Alfred Wegener

Words to Know

Continental drift:
The theory that continents move apart slowly at a predictable rate.

Convection currents:
Circular movement of a fluid in response to alternating heating and cooling.

Crust:
The hard outer shell of Earth that floats upon the softer, denser mantle.

Lava:
Molten rock that occurs at the surface of Earth, usually through volcanic eruptions.

Words to Know

Magma:
Molten rock deep within Earth that consists of liquids, gases, and particles of rocks and crystals. Magma underlies areas of volcanic activity and at Earth's surface is called lava.

Magma chambers:
Pools of bubbling liquid rock that are the source of energy causing volcanoes to be active.

Magma surge:
A swell or rising wave of magma caused by the movement and friction of tectonic plates, which heats and melts rock, adding to the magma and its force.

(1880–1930) proposed that the continents were moving apart slowly at a predictable rate. He coined the term **continental drift** and conducted much research to support his theory. Many thought Wegener's idea was radical, but his suggestion that some force caused the continents to move eventually became the key to unlocking the dynamics of a volcano.

After Wegener died, the geologists who agreed with his theory took it a step further. They proposed that the radioactive decay of naturally occuring elements deep within Earth produced tremendous heat. The heat was so intense that it melted rock, forming a vast caldron of liquid that boiled and swirled in vast amounts. This bubbling mass generated **convection currents,** currents of molten rock. The scientists suggested that these molten rock currents pushed up under ridges in the ocean and through active volcanoes—moving the continents.

How does a volcano blow its top?

Deep under a volcano is Earth's **mantle,** a layer that lies between the the Earth's **crust** or outermost layer, which extends 25 miles (40 kilometers) down, and Earth's **core.** The further down, the hotter the temperature gets. Earth's inner core can reach 13,000°F (7,000°C). At the top of the mantle, around 30 miles (45 kilometers) down, **magma** can be found. Magma is liquid rock that consists of gases and silica; this substance collects and forms pools known as a **magma chambers,**—which are the volcano's furnace. The gases bubble through the magma, making the liquid hotter and lighter than surrounding rocks, and this helps push this volatile liquid mixture up through a volcano's vent.

Even the slight strain of tides can affect the inner pressure of a volcano and cause it to blow. Most often, though, the cause is the move-

ment of **tectonic plates**, large flat pieces of rocks that form Earth's outer crust and fit together like pieces of a cracked eggshell. Grinding or overlapping can melt some of the plate rock, which pushes it up into the magma chamber, where it causes a **magma surge.** If the dome over a volcano's vent is obstructed with rock or dirt, pressure builds up even more, causing a more violent eruption. The same basic principles that govern tectonic plate movement can cause both earthquakes and volcanic eruptions, so it is not surprising that both can be detected by the same instrument. While **seismographs** are used mostly for detecting earthquakes, they can also detect vibrations deep within Earth that indicate the gradual rise of magma.

Sometimes there's a good side to a down side

The citizens of Pompeii and others who died because of volcanic eruptions would certainly disagree that there is any positive side to this natural disaster; but volcanic eruptions do have some good effects. If an eruption produces a layer of ash less than 8 inches (20 centimeters) thick, farmers get a free, nutrient-rich natural fertilizer blanketing

Words to Know

Mantle:
Thick dense layer of rock that underlies Earth's crust and overlies the core.

Seismograph:
A device that records vibrations of the ground and within Earth.

Seismometer:
A seismograph that measures the movement of the ground.

experiment
CENTRAL

their land. For example, the ash from Mount Vesuvius helps the grapes grow in that area's wine region. Although the 20 feet (6 meters) of ash that covered Pompeii smothered every living thing, the ash also preserved the city, its artifacts, and its inhabitants. Archeological findings have shown us in detail the civilization of an ancient people who were lively, cultured, and gifted.

In the following projects you will be able to learn more about volcanoes.

Project 1
Model of a Volcano: Will it blow its top?

Purpose
In this activity you will construct a working model of a volcano. This model will demonstrate the dynamics of magma flow and the gaseous buildup that causes a volcano to blow.

Level of Difficulty
Moderate.

Materials Needed
- glue
- 8-inch (20-centimeter) long plastic tube, 1.5 inches (3.8 centimeter) in diameter
- 4 plastic straws
- newspaper
- masking tape
- scissors
- 4 rolls plaster of Paris gauze (or papier-maché mix and newspaper)
- empty film container
- effervescent antacid tablets
- water
- goggles or other eye protection
- brown and red water-based or acrylic paint
- cornstarch
- baking soda
- vinegar
- red food coloring

Words to Know

Tectonic plates:
Huge flat rocks that form Earth's crust.

Volcano:
A conical mountain or dome of lava, ash, and cinders that forms around a vent leading to molten rock deep within Earth.

Approximate Budget

$10 to $15.

Timetable

2 to 3 hours.

Step-by-Step Instructions

1. Place about six sheets of newspaper over the surface you will be working on.

Step 3: Set-up of plastic tube and straws.

Steps 4 and 5: Wrap newspaper sticks around the tube, making sure the straws stick out, and tape into place.

How to Work Safely

Do not activate the volcano's eruption without adult supervision. Wear goggles to do it. Always handle scissors carefully.

2. Poke four holes in the plastic tube between 1 and 2 inches (2.5 to 5 centimeters) from the bottom. Make sure the straws can fit through the holes.

3. Glue the straws into the tube's holes, making sure the glue does not clog the straws' openings.

4. Twist a sheet of newspaper into a stick shape. Repeat with several sheets.

5. Wrap the sticks around the tube, making sure the straws stick out, and tape into place. The bottom should be wide and the top narrower, just like a volcano.

6. Gently moisten the plaster of Paris strips and wrap them around the volcano. Make sure you cover all the newspaper.

7. Allow to dry for 30 minutes. Trim the straws that are protruding out of the volcano.

8. Paint the surface with brown and red water-based or acrylic paint and allow to dry.

9. Using leftover material, create a cap that covers the top of the plastic tube. Make sure it's removable but snug.

10. Remove the volcano cap.

11. Place one to five antacid tablets inside the plastic film container

12. Pour 1 tablespoon of water into the container. Snap the top on and drop into the plastic tube opening at the top of the volcano.

13. Place the volcano cap back on quickly, stand back, and watch it blow!

14. Remove the volcano cap.

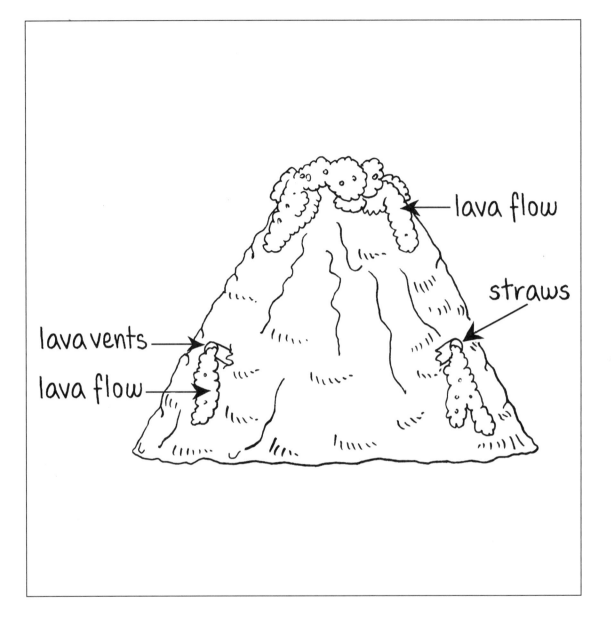

lava flow

straws

lava vents

lava flow

Step 16: The magma mixture will swell inside the volcano and cause a bubbling eruption. Slowly the magma will creep out of the volcano and become lava.

15. Mix 1 cup (224 grams) of cornstarch with 0.75 cup (178 milliliters) of water. Add ten drops of red food coloring. Add 0.25 cup (56 grams) baking soda mix and add 0.25 cup (56 grams) of vinegar.

16. Pour the mixture into the plastic tube and observe. The magma mixture will swell inside the volcano and cause a bubbling eruption. Slowly the magma will creep out of the volcano and become lava. Lava should also slowly come out of the straw vents on the side.

experiment
CENTRAL

Troubleshooter's Guide

Here are some problems that may arise during this project, possible causes, and ways to remedy the problems.

Problem: The magma/lava flow did not come out of the straws.

Possible cause: The tubes are clogged. Stick a pipe cleaner through the straws to make sure the tubes are open. Add more vinegar and baking soda to the mix and try again.

Problem: The film container did not blow the top off the volcano.

Possible cause: You need more antacid. Try adding more to the container and do not forget to wear your goggles.

Summary of Results

Write a paragraph explaining what you witnessed when the volcano erupted and the magama/lava flowed. Research how Mount Vesuvius blew and compare your volcano with how that volcano erupted. Make a diagram of the internal structure of the volcano.

Project 2
Looking at a Seismograph: Can a volcanic eruption be detected?

Purpose

Seismometers are instruments that detect disturbances in Earth's crust. Used mostly for earthquake detection, they can also measure the turbulence of a volcano's magma activity. The disturbance or activity is recorded on a seismograph, a sheet of paper that shows the intensity of the activity. For this project you will construct a seismograph that will simulate the types of disturbances that indicate volcanic activity.

Level of Difficulty

Easy.

experiment
CENTRAL

Materials Needed

- shoe box
- metal coil toy (like a Slinky)
- metal block (or a stone), 2 by 2 inches (5 x 5 centimeters)
- pencil
- roll of adding machine tape
- scissors
- tape

Approximate Budget

$2 to $5 for purchase of coil toy and adding machine tape.

Timetable

Less than 30 minutes.

Step-by-Step Instructions

1. Cut a 2.5 to 3-inch (6 to 7-centimeter) slit on each side of a shoe box.

2. With scissors cut the coil toy in half.

3. Poke a hole in the top of the box and pull a few coils of the toy through.

4. Tape the metal block to the spring.

5. Tape the pencil to the block. Face the tip toward the back and make sure the tip touches the back wall.

6. Carefully feed the paper through both slits cut in the side walls. Do not tear the paper. You have now built the seismograph.

7. Place your seismograph on a table.

How to Work Safely

Handle scissors carefully.

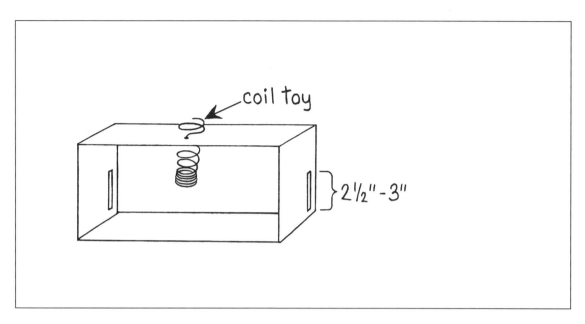

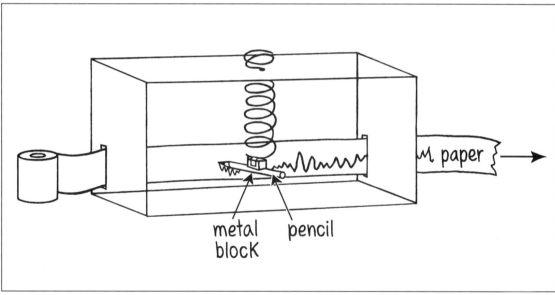

8. Place any heavy object on top of the seismograph to hold it in place.

9. Ask a friend to help by gently shaking the table or lifting it off the ground a half inch.

10. As your friend is causing the disturbance, slowly and gently pull the paper through the hole.

TOP: Steps 1 to 3: Set-up of shoe box and coil toy.

BOTTOM: Steps 4 to 6: Set-up of the seismograph.

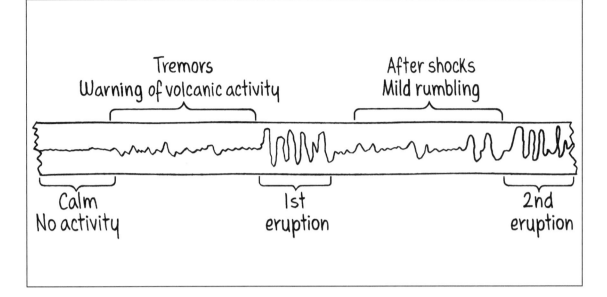

Tremors
Warning of volcanic activity

After shocks
Mild rumbling

Calm
No activity

1st
eruption

2nd
eruption

Sample seismograph paper with observations recorded. How does your paper compare?

Summary of Results

Examine your seismic data. The tape records the magnitude of seismic disturbances in Earth's crust that can lead to a magma surge. Mark your tape with observations of what may have happened if a volcano really erupted. Refer to the illustration, above, of the sample seismograph paper for ideas.

Troubleshooter's Guide

Here are some problems that may arise during this experiment, some possible causes, and ways to remedy the problems.

Problem: The pencil does not move up and down.

Possible cause: The coil toy is too tight. Either try a heavier coil toy or gently stretch the coil toy until the coils no longer touch each other.

Problem: The pencil is not making clear marks on the seismograph paper.

Possible cause: The pencil is not touching the paper. Adjust it or try using a marker with a fine tip.

Design Your Own Experiment

How to Select a Topic Relating to this Concept

These projects are simple models that will familiarize you with some of the important dynamics of a volcano. If you wish to investigate further, research the type, sizes, and places of volcanoes. Or lava flows, properties of lava, or the effects of volcanic ash may interest you.

Check the For More Information section and talk with your science teacher or school or community media specialist to start gathering information on volcano questions that interest you.

Steps in the Scientific Method

To do an original experiment, you need to plan carefully and think things through. Otherwise, you might not be sure what question you are answering, what you are or should be measuring, or what your findings prove or disprove.

Here are the steps in designing an experiment:

- State the purpose of—and the underlying question behind—the experiment you propose to do.
- Recognize the variables involved, and select one that will help you answer the question at hand.
- State a testable hypothesis, an educated guess about the answer to your question.
- Decide how to change the variable you selected.
- Decide how to measure your results

Recording Data and Summarizing the Results

In any experiment, you should keep notes and data organized so that others can utilize and understand it. Charts, graphs, and pictures are excellent ways to share and summarize your results.

Related Projects

Besides constructing a model of a volcano and simulating its eruption, you could investigate the environmental effects of eruptions or past climate changes due to eruptions. Start by asking a question you want answered. Then construct an investigation around that question.

For More Information

Van Rose, Susanna. *Volcano & Earthquake.* New York: Knopf, 1992. ❖ Photographs and text explain the causes and effects of volcanoes and earthquakes and examine specific occurrences throughout history.

chapter 46

Properties of Water

Without water, the life forms we see on Earth could not possibly exist. This simple combination of three atoms—one oxygen, two hydrogen—acts in complex ways that can turn a barren, dusty planet into a thriving biological community. What are the properties of water that make it so versatile and vital? How can we measure and compare water's properties to those of other liquids?

A number of observable properties of water result from its molecular structure, meaning not only the atoms that make up water, but also the shape of the water molecule. The bonds between the one oxygen and two hydrogen atoms do not form a straight line but form an angle like a wide *V.* This shape gives the molecule a positive electric charge on one side and a negative electric charge on the other. This charge gives water the properties of **adhesion,** the tendency to stick to certain other substances and **cohesion,** the tendency to stick to itself.

Adhesion and cohesion in everyday life

The properties of adhesion and cohesion can be easily observed by watching raindrops on a windowpane. Adhesion holds the drops to the glass. Even if the window is tilted forward, some drops will cling to the underside of the pane. Cohesion can be seen if you trace the path of drops down the pane. Drops close to one another will be drawn together by cohesion, forming larger drops. Observe carefully and you will see that drops will far more readily join together than split apart. Splitting a water drop requires some energy or change to loosen the bonds that hold the molecules together.

Words to Know

Adhesion:
Attraction between two different substances.

Buoyancy:
The tendency of a liquid to exert a lifting effect on a body immersed in it.

Capillary Action:
The tendency of water to rise through a narrow tube by the force of adhesion between the water and the walls of the tube.

Cohesion:
Attraction between like substances.

experiment
CENTRAL

*The molecular
structure of water.*

HYDROGEN   +   HYDROGEN

                OXYGEN

                −

*Water's adhesive force
causes its meniscus to
rise up the walls of the
straw. Mercury's cohesive
force causes it to bow
away from the walls of
the straw and toward itself.
(Photo Researchers Inc.
Reproduced by permission.)*

ⓦords to Know

Density:
The mass of a substance compared to its volume.

Hydrophilic:
A substance that is attracted to and readily mixes with water.

Hydrophobic:
A substance that is repelled by and does not mix with water.

Cohesion, as you might predict, results from the attraction of one water molecule's positive side to another water molecule's negative side. Cohesion creates **surface tension,** which enables water bugs to "skate" along the water's surface without sinking. The first experiment will demonstrate that surface tension can keep afloat an object that is denser than water. You will then compare the surface tension of two other liquids to that of water.

Forces affecting adhesion

Adhesion, water's tendency to cling to certain substances, creates **capillary action.** In extremely narrow spaces, such as inside water vessels in the stem of a plant, water will actually rise against gravity by the force of adhesion. This capillary action helps plants pull water up from the soil.

Cohesion, the bonding of water molecules to one another, enables this water bug to "skate" over the water's surface without sinking. (Peter Arnold Inc. Reproduced by permission.)

Observe the surface of water in a straw: the water can be seen "climbing" the wall of the straw. This bowing of the water's surface is called the **meniscus,** and it is caused by the strength of the water's adhesion to the solid around it. In liquids that have much stronger cohesion than adhesion, such as mercury, the meniscus bows upward at the middle and down at the edges.

Adhesion in water depends upon the structure of the second substance's molecules. Some substances are **hydrophilic,** attracted to water, and some are **hydrophobic,** not attracted to water. This explains why water will easily clean a salty film off your hands, but will not efficiently remove grease without using detergent. Salt is hydrophilic, but grease is normally hydrophobic. Detergent acts as a link between the water molecules and the grease. The molecules of the detergent possess one end that bonds with the grease and another end that bonds with water. When these detergent molecules coat the grease, they change it from hydrophobic to hydrophilic (see illustration on page 700).

In the first experiment, you will demonstrate the strength of the cohesive force of water by floating a metal object (one that ordinarily would not float) on its surface. In the second experiment, you will measure the adhesive force between water and a solid by determining how much weight is required to break the strength of adhesion.

(see illustration on page 700).

Words to Know

Hypothesis:
An idea in the form of a statement that can be tested by observation and/or experiment.

Meniscus:
The curved surface of a column of liquid.

Variable:
Anything that might affect the results of an experiment.

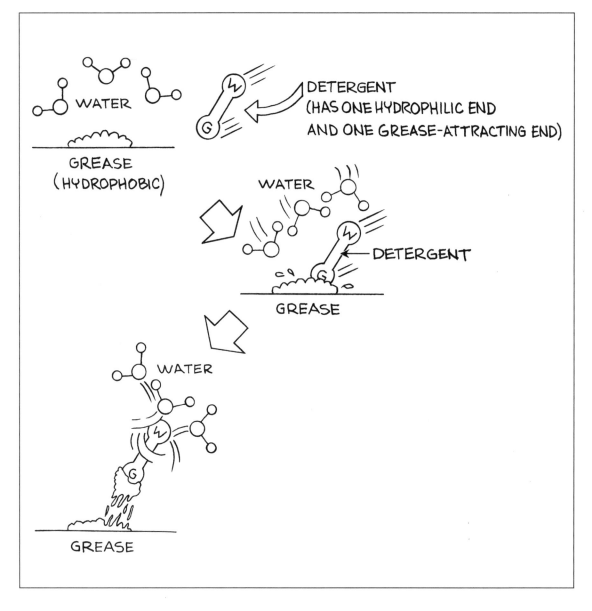

WATER

GREASE
(HYDROPHOBIC)

DETERGENT
(HAS ONE HYDROPHILIC END
AND ONE GREASE-ATTRACTING END)

WATER

DETERGENT

GREASE

WATER

GREASE

The action of detergent between water and grease.

You will then predict how coating the solid with a hydrophobic substance such as grease or petroleum jelly will affect the strength of adhesion.

experiment
CENTRAL

Experiment 1

Cohesion: Can the cohesive force of surface tension in water support an object denser than water?

Purpose/Hypothesis

In this experiment, you will first demonstrate the strength of the cohesive force of water by floating a metal object on its surface. Then you will test the relative cohesive force of two other liquids by attempting to float the same object and others on them. Before you begin, make an educated guess about the outcome of this experiment based on your knowledge of the properties of water. This educated guess, or prediction, is your **hypothesis.** A hypothesis should explain these things:

- the topic of the experiment
- the variable you will change
- the variable you will measure
- what you expect to happen

A hypothesis should be brief, specific, and measurable. It must be something you can test through observation. Your experiment will prove or disprove whether your hypothesis is correct. Here is one pos-

What Are the Variables?

Variables are anything that might affect the results of an experiment. Here are the main variables in this experiment:

- the composition of the liquids

- the purity of the liquids

- the type of objects used to test surface tension

- the method by which the objects are placed on the liquids

In other words, the variables in this experiment are everything that might affect the surface tension of the liquid. If you change more than one variable, you will not be able to tell which variable had the most effect on surface tension.

sible hypothesis for this experiment: "We can determine from observation of surface tension whether other liquids have greater or lesser cohesion than water."

In this case, the **variable** you will change is the liquid, and the variable you will measure is whether the object floats or sinks. You expect that you will be able to observe the differences in surface tension between liquids.

Level of Difficulty

Easy/moderate.

Materials Needed

- 3 wide-mouth glass jars or drinking glasses
- corn oil
- isopropyl alcohol
- distilled water
- 3 unused staples (make sure they are clean of any adhesive)
- 3 small sewing needles
- 3 small steel paper clips
- 3 large steel paper clips
- tweezers
- safety goggles

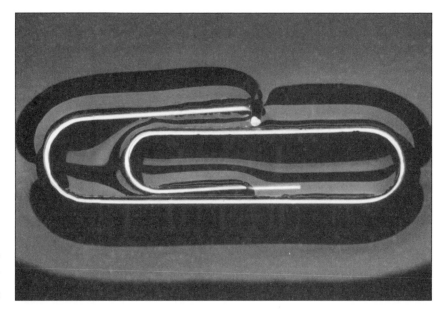

Surface tension of a paper clip floating on water. (Photo Researchers Inc. Reproduced by permission.)

How to Experiment Safely

Do not substitute any other liquids in this experiment without checking with your teacher first. Always wear goggles when experimenting with alcohol and work in a well-ventilated room. Keep the alcohol away from your nose and mouth.

Approximate Budget

$1 to $10. (Most materials may be found in the average household.)

Timetable

10 to 20 minutes.

Step-by-Step Instructions

1. Pour 2 inches (5 centimeters) of water into jar 1. Fill jar 2 to the same level with alcohol, and fill jar 3 to the same level with oil.

2. If you are using objects other that those in the materials list, make sure none of them is less dense than the liquid, which would make them float due to **buoyancy** and not due to cohesion and surface tension. To find out, push each object to the bottom of the liquid. If it floats to the top, then you must replace it with something denser.

Step 5: Sample data chart for Experiment 1.

	staple	needle	sm. paper clip	lg. paper clip
cup one	floats	floats	sinks	sinks
cup two				
cup three				

experiment
CENTRAL

3. Using the tweezers, carefully place a staple flat on the surface of the water. You should have little difficulty floating the staple on the water.

4. Remove the staple and try the needle and the paper clips. Do not put two objects in the cup at the same time, and let any ripples settle before trying the next object.

5. On your chart, describe what each object does. Your chart should look something like the illustration on page 703.

6. Repeat steps 3, 4, and 5 with jar 2 and jar 3.

Summary of Results

Examine your chart and compare the results of the tests for each liquid. Did your predictions prove true? Were you able to get meaningful results for each liquid? Which liquid had the strongest cohesion? The weakest? How did the cohesive force of alcohol and oil compare to the cohesion of water?

Change the Variables

You can change the variables and conduct similar experiments. For example, what happens to the surface tension if you dissolve salt in the

Troubleshooter's Guide

When doing experiments in adhesion and cohesion, be aware that unintended impurities can greatly affect your results. Natural oil from your fingers can alter the behavior of a small object on water, and an invisible soap film on the inside of a glass can easily spoil your results. Here is a problem that may arise during this experiment, some possible causes, and ways to remedy the problem:

Problem: When any object is placed on the surface of the water, it sinks.

Possible causes:

1. None of your objects is light enough. Try using a staple and a sewing needle.

2. Your water has been contaminated. Dump it out, clean the glass, and make sure the glass is rinsed clean of any soap residue.

experiment
CENTRAL

water? That is, does salty seawater have a different surface tension than fresh water? You can also change the temperature of the water—either cooling or heating it—to determine the effect on surface tension. Warning: Do not try heating the alcohol, as it may burn with an almost-invisible flame and cause injury or damage.

Experiment 2
Adhesion: How much weight is required to break the adhesive force between an object and water?

Purpose/Hypothesis
In this experiment, you will first determine the strength of the adhesive force between a flat piece of wood and the surface of water. Then you will measure the effect of altering the adhesion between the two by adding a hydrophobic substance. Before you begin, make an educated guess about the outcome of this experiment based on your knowledge of the properties of water. This educated guess, or prediction, is your **hypothesis.** A hypothesis should explain these things:

• the topic of the experiment
• the variable you will change
• the variable you will measure
• what you expect to happen

A hypothesis should be brief, specific, and measurable. It must be something you can test through observation. Your experiment will prove or disprove whether your hypothesis is correct. Here is one possible hypothesis for this experiment: "A coating of a hydrophobic substance on an object will measurably reduce the adhesive force between that object and water."

In this case, the **variable** you will change is the coating on the object, and the variable you will measure is amount of weight (force) it takes to overcome the surface tension. You expect that a hydrophobic coating on an object will reduce the weight required to overcome surface tension.

Level of Difficulty
Easy/moderate.

What Are the Variables?

Variables are anything that might affect the results of an experiment. Here are the main variables in this experiment:

• the purity of the water

• the shape of the object used to test adhesion

• the type of substance applied to the object

• the amount of substance applied to the object

In other words, the variables in this experiment are everything that might affect the surface tension of the liquid. If you change more than one variable, you will not be able to tell which variable had the most effect on surface tension.

Materials Needed

• 9 x 12-inch (23 x 30-centimeter) pan
• block of balsa wood, approximately 6 inches (15 centimeters) square and less than 1 inch (2.5 centimeters) thick, available in most hobby stores)
• 12-inch (30-centimeter) or longer wooden dowel
• wooden ruler with three holes (to fit a three-ring binder)
• plastic container with two holes punched near the lip
• thumb tacks
• string
• pencil
• distilled water
• 0.25-cup of a hydrophobic substance such as cooking oil, grease, or petroleum jelly
• 5 rolls of pennies (or enough to fill the container)

Approximate Budget

$10 to $15. (Most materials may be found in the average household.)

Timetable

1 to 2 hours.

Step-by-Step Instructions

1. Assemble your balance.

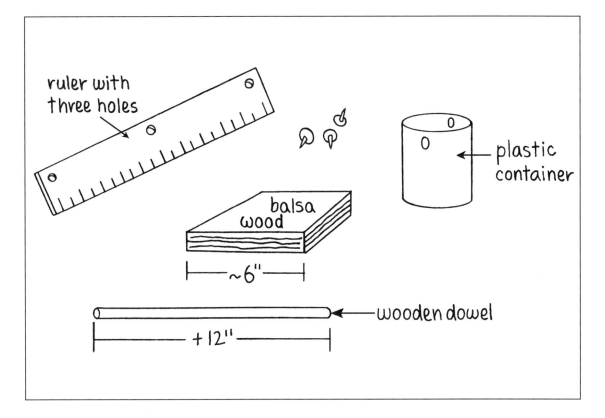

a. Measure and mark the exact center of the block of wood (draw two diagonals from corner to corner). Cut a 30-inch (76-centimeter) length of string and tie a small loop in one end. Push a thumb tack partway into the center mark. Twist the loop of string around the tack, and push the tack as far into the wood as possible, securing the string.

b. Cut a 24-inch (60-centimeter) length of string and loop the end through the two holes in the lip of the plastic container. Then

The materials pictured will serve to test your hypothesis, but you might wish to construct a sturdier set-up for demonstrations or repeated tests.

How to Experiment Safely

Do not substitute any other substances in this experiment without checking with your science teacher first. If you decide to construct a sturdier balance, remember that you must wear safety glasses when hammering nails.

TOP: *Steps 1 to 3: The assembled balance should look like this.*

BOTTOM: *Step 4: Sample data chart for Experiment 2.*

tie the end onto the length of string about 4 inches (10 centimeters) up from the container.

c. Cut a 6-inch (15-centimeter) length of string and tie it firmly around the dowel, 2 inches (5 centimeters) from the end. If necessary, put a tack next to the loop of string to keep it from slipping off. Tie the other end of the string through the center hole of the ruler.

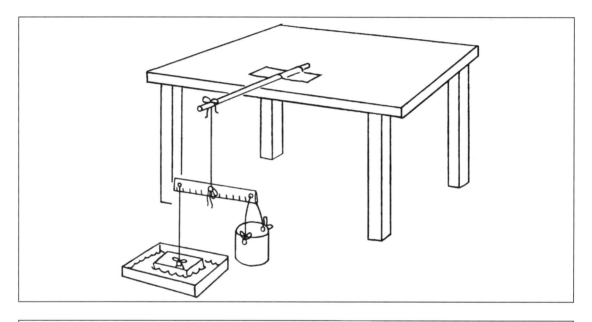

	Trial #1	Trial #2	Trial #3
uncoated block	112 pennies	105 pennies	
block w/ hydrophobic substance			

d. Place the dowel on a desk so the ruler is suspended at least 6 inches (15 centimeters) out over the floor. Attach the wooden block's string to one of the outside holes on the ruler. Make sure that when the ruler is held level, the block is suspended 1 inch (2.5 centimeters) from the floor.

2. Attach the plastic container to the other end of the ruler and begin filling it with pennies until the weight is balanced. Record how many pennies equals the weight of the wood block.

3. Place the pan on the floor beneath the wood block. Fill the pan with water until the block is resting on the water's surface. The ruler should remain at or close to level. (You may need someone to steady the ruler so it does not shift from side to side during this step.)

4. Begin adding pennies to the plastic container until the downward force of the weight overcomes the force of adhesion and lifts the block off the surface of the water. Record the number of pennies added on a chart like the one illustrated on page 708.

5. Wipe the block and let it sit in a warm place for several hours until it is dry. Coat the underside of the block with your hydrophobic substance. (Note: Once you have coated the block, you will not be able to repeat Step 4. Some of the substance may remain permanently on the wood, changing the adhesive force. If you wish to do repeated tests, you must use two blocks.)

6. Remove enough pennies so the block is balanced once more, and place the block back on the water's surface. Repeat Step 4. Record the number of pennies necessary to lift the block clear of the water.

Summary of Results

Examine your data and compare the results of the tests with your hypothesis. Did your hypothesis prove true? Compare the number of pennies necessary to balance the block in step 2 to the number necessary to break the surface tension in step 4. The difference between these two numbers shows the strength of the surface tension. Note on your chart the exact number of pennies.

Change the Variables

You can vary this experiment to investigate different aspects of adhesion and cohesion. Try altering the test materials to determine whether different solids have different levels of adhesion to water. Repeat the

experiment
CENTRAL

Troubleshooter's Guide

When doing experiments in adhesion and cohesion, be aware that unintended impurities can greatly affect your results. Natural oil from your fingers can alter the behavior of a small object on water, and an invisible soap film on the inside of a container can easily spoil your results. Here are some problems that may arise during this experiment, some possible causes, and ways to remedy the problems:

Problem: The block breaks free of the adhesive force after the addition of very little or no weight.

Possible cause: The tack in the block is not properly centered. Pulling upward on one side of the block will overcome the adhesive force more easily. Center the tack.

Problem: The plastic container is full and the block still has not been balanced or lifted.

Possible causes:

1. Your container is too small.

2. Your block is too heavy. Use balsa wood (and not a hardwood).

experiment using a block wrapped in plastic and another wrapped in aluminum foil. Hypothesize whether the two will show different levels of adhesion and test your hypothesis. Be sure to check with your teacher before testing with new materials.

 **Design Your Own Experiment**

How to Select a Topic Relating to this Concept

The simple experiments described here touch on only a few aspects of adhesion and cohesion. Many experiments on the nature of hydrophilic and hydrophobic substances can be performed with inexpensive, readily available materials.

Check the For More Information section and talk with your science teacher or school or community media specialist to start gathering information on water property questions that interest you.

Steps in the Scientific Method

To do an original experiment, you need to plan carefully and think things through. Otherwise, you might not be sure what question you are answering, what you are or should be measuring, or what your findings prove or disprove.

Here are the steps in designing an experiment:

- State the purpose of—and the underlying question behind—the experiment you propose to do.
- Recognize the variables involved, and select one that will help you answer the question at hand.
- State a testable hypothesis, an educated guess about the answer to your question.
- Decide how to change the variable you have selected.
- Decide how to measure your results.

Recording Data and Summarizing the Results

In the experiments included here and in any experiments you develop, you can look for ways to display your data in more accurate and interesting ways. Diagrams would be especially useful in Experiment 2.

Remember that those who view your results may not have seen the experiment performed, so you must present the information you have gathered in as clear a way as possible. Including photographs or illustrations of the steps in the experiment is a good way to show a viewer how you got from your hypothesis to your conclusion.

Related Projects

To develop other experiments on this topic, think about adhesion and cohesion in everyday life. Why does a coaster stick to the bottom of a wet glass? Investigate the function of capillary action in plants. Think of ways you could demonstrate the reason oil spills are so damaging to our ecosystem. Investigate how oil spills are cleaned up without polluting the water with detergents.

For More Information

Ray, C. Claibourne. *The New York Times Book of Science Questions and Answers.* New York: Doubleday, 1997. ❖ Addresses both everyday observations and advanced scientific concepts on a wide variety of subjects.

Van Cleave, Janice. *Chemistry For Every Kid.* New York: John Wiley and Sons, Inc., 1989. ❖ Contains a number of simple and informative demonstrations and investigations into properties of water, including cohesion, the meniscus, and capillary action.

chapter 47

Rivers of Water

The Carson begins in California, rushing northward from the head-waters on Sonora Peak in the Sierra Nevada Mountains, then rambling through gorges and alpine meadows. After leaving California, its next destination is the desert plain of Nevada. The Carson is a **river,** a main course of water into which many smaller bodies of water flow. The longest river in North America is the Mississippi. At 2,280 miles (3670 kilometers), it's the tenth longest on Earth. The Nile River, the world champion in length, winds 4,145 miles (6670 kilometers) from the equator to the Mediterranean Sea.

First things first

The source of a river's waters, in fact, all the waters of the world, is the **hydrologic cycle,** which circulates and distributes the fresh water on Earth. To examine this cycle, we might begin with the sea. The Sun warms the ocean water, causing some of the surface water to evaporate and rise into the air as water vapor. Upon meeting cooler air above, this water vapor condenses and forms rain droplets, or it freezes into ice crystals. The droplets or crystals eventually fall again as precipitation: rain, snow, or hail. Some precipitation falls back into the sea, while some falls on land where it sinks into the ground, or runs into rivers, lakes, ponds, and streams.

French scientist Claude Perrault was one of the first to describe the hydrologic or water cycle. In 1674, he measured the precipitation that fell into the upper Seine River's basin and compared it with the esti-mated amount of water flowing into the Seine from streams and small-

Words to Know

Braided rivers:
Wide, shallow rivers with multiple channels and pebbly islands in the middle.

Channel:
A shallow trench carved into the ground by the pressure and movement of a river.

Control experiment:
A set-up that is identical to the experiment but is not affected by the vari-able that will be changed during the experiment.

The Maruia River on South Island, New Zealand, is a meandering river. (Corbis-Bettmann. Reproduced by permission.)

er rivers. The precipitation added about six times as much water as the streams. This was a significant discovery because previously scientists had thought that all rivers were fed by underground springs.

Mapping out the journey

Rivers begin in mountains as several streams. These streams are formed from runoff consisting of rain, melted snow, sleet, and hail, as well as underground water that rises to the surface. Smaller streams gather into larger streams until they form a river. The river makes its home in a **channel,** a shallow trench carved into the ground from the pressure, volume, and movement of the water.

The journey of a river is rarely straight. Wide, shallow rivers with pebbly islands in the middle are called **braided rivers.** The islands split the river into many streams, which then come together again, just like braided hair. Lowland rivers that twist and turn before flowing to the sea are called **meandering** rivers. The term originated from the Latin word *maeander.* For example, the Menderes River in Turkey is famous for its windy course. Scotland's Deveron River meanders 26 miles (42

OPPOSITE PAGE:
The Nile River plays an important part in the hydrologic cycle. (Peter Arnold Inc. Reproduced by permission.)

experiment
CENTRAL

The Niagara River and its falls have carved out a 100-foot (30-meter) deep plunge pool. (Photo Researchers Inc. Reproduced by permission.)

kilometers) back and forth across the land, but its actual straight-line length is only 6.5 miles (10.5 kilometers).

The power of water

Where does a river's energy come from? The elevation of the land triggers its push, even in areas where the slope is gentle. The speed and volume of a river descending a steep slope can reshape Earth's surface, picking up soil and rocky debris and then dropping it when the water

experiment
CENTRAL

slows down and loses some of its energy. Rivers have gouged out canyons, built mud and stone landforms, and sculpted solid rock into pillars and arches.

An example of how powerful a river's force can be is the Niagara River, which runs through Canada and the United States. As it courses downslope on its 35-mile (56-kilometer) trail, the water pounds everything along its way. The cliff that creates its falls is a ridge made of dolomite, a very tough limestone. The river has worn down the ridge's overlying rock, creating a lower area that focuses the fall of the water.

In the following two experiments, you will explore ways that water changes the shape of our environment. The experiments will help you appreciate how rivers and streams have influenced the shape of your own community.

Experiment 1
Weathering Erosion in Glaciers: How does a river make a trench?

Purpose/Hypothesis

In this experiment you will investigate the effects that **glaciers**, rivers of ice, have on the landscape, such as forming trenches and **moraines**, arc-shaped ridges of rocky debris. Before you begin, make an educated guess about the outcome of this experiment based on your knowledge of glaciers. This educated guess, or prediction, is your **hypothesis**. A hypothesis should explain these things:

- the topic of the experiment
- the variable you will change
- the variable you will measure
- what you expect to happen

A hypothesis should be brief, specific, and measurable. It must be something you can test through observation. Your experiment will prove or disprove whether your hypothesis is correct. Here is one possible hypothesis for this experiment: "Ice flow causes sediment erosion."

In this case, the **variable** you will change is the presence of an ice flow, and the variable you will measure is the movement of soil in the ice flow's path. You expect the ice flow to cause erosion.

What Are the Variables?

Variables are anything that might affect the results of an experiment. Here are the main variables in this experiment:

- size of the ice flow
- size of pieces of sediment
- temperature surrounding ice flow
- duration of the experiment

In other words, the variables in this experiment are everything that might affect the sediment erosion. If you change more than one variable, you will not be able to tell which variable had the most effect on erosion.

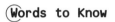

Words to Know

Moraine:
Mass of boulders, stones, and other rock debris carried along and deposited by a glacier.

River: A main course of water into which many other smaller bodies of water flow.

Sediment:
Sand, silt, clay, rock, gravel, mud, or other matter that has been transported by flowing water.

Variable:
Something that can affect the results of an experiment.

As a **control experiment,** you will set up one tray of sand with no ice flow in it. That way, you can determine whether the sand moves even with no ice flow. If the sand moves under the ice flow, but not in the control tray, your hypothesis will be supported.

Level of Difficulty
Moderate.

Materials Needed
- 10 pounds (4.5 kilograms) play sand for sandboxes
- 24-inch (60-centimeter) square of window screening
- two 8 x 24-inch (20 x 61-centimeter) plastic trays (Liners for window boxes are ideal.)
- water
- freezer
- ruler
- bucket

Approximate Budget
$15.

Timetable
30 minutes to set up; 5 minutes a day to add water over a 30-day period.

Step-by-Step Instructions

1. Place the screening over the bucket and sift the sand by pouring it through the screen. Save any sand that remains on the screen. Discard any sand that goes through the screen.

2. Pour the sand that remained on the screen into both plastic trays.

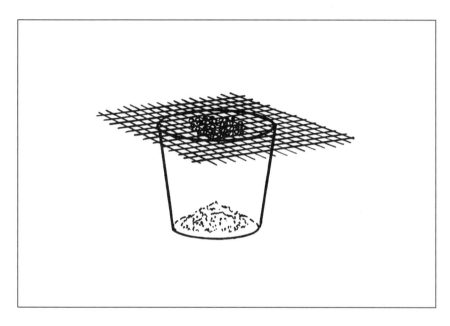

Step 1: Screening over the bucket.

Step 5: Place the trays inside the freezer and prop up the ends with the well about 1 inch.

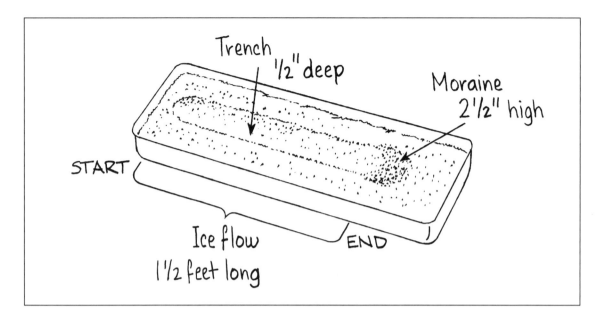

Trench
½" deep

Moraine
2½" high

START

Ice flow
1½ feet long

END

Steps 10 and 11:
Tray showing pattern
left by ice flow.

3. Using the side of the ruler, smooth the surface of the sand in the trays and measure the depth of the sand. Make sure the sand is the same depth in both trays.

4. Using your finger, make a well in the sand at one end of both plastic trays.

5. Place the trays inside the freezer and prop up the ends with the well about 1 inch (2.5 centimeters).

6. Pour 0.25 cup (60 milliliters) of water into the well of one tray (the experimental tray) and close the door. The control tray will have no water—and thus no ice. Add another 0.25 cup (60 milliliters) of water to the experimental tray daily for 30 days.

7. After 30 days, record the length of the ice flow that formed in the experimental tray.

8. Carefully remove both trays from the freezer.

9. Allow the ice flow to melt 6 to 12 hours.

10. Diagram the pattern the ice caused in the sand; describe the sand pattern in the control tray.

11. Measure the depth of the sand in the trench and at the end of the ice flow in the experimental tray. Measure the sand depth at both ends of the control tray. Record your findings.

Troubleshooter's Guide

Here is a problem that may arise during this experiment, some possible causes, and ways to remedy the problem.

Problem: After 10 days, there is no ice accumulation near the well in the experimental tray. All the water flows quickly through the sand to the bottom of the tray.

Possible causes:

1. The angle is too steep. Lower both trays to a very gentle slope.

2. The sand is too coarse. Try a finer mesh screen and use smaller grains of sand.

Summary of Results

Organize your data on a chart that shows the sand levels in both trays at the beginning and the end of the experiment. Compare your end results. Did the ice flow move sediment? Did erosion take place in the control tray? Write a paragraph summarizing what you found.

Change the Variables

You can change the variables in this experiment by using different soils. You might try top soil or a more rocky soil. Also, you can change the angle of the slope and see how the depth of the trench is affected. Gravity plays a large role in soil movement. The steeper the slope, the greater the pull of gravity.

Experiment 2
Stream Flow: Does the stream meander?

Purpose/Hypothesis

Rivers and streams can carve patterns into Earth's surface. This experiment will simulate the force that water can have in an environment. Will a water travel in a straight path down a slope? Before you begin, make an educated guess about the outcome of this experiment based

What Are the Variables?

Variables are anything that might affect the results of an experiment. Here are the main variables in this experiment:

- the kind of soil being used (size and composition)
- the flowrate of water used
- the slope of the landscape
- the duration of the water flow

In other words, the variables in this experiment are everything that might affect the stream pattern. If you change more than one variable, you will not be able to tell which variable had the most effect on the pattern.

on your knowledge of stream patterns. This educated guess, or prediction, is your **hypothesis.** A hypothesis should explain these things:

- the topic of the experiment
- the variable you will change
- the variable you will measure
- what you expect to happen

A hypothesis should be brief, specific, and measurable. It must be something you can test through observation. Your experiment will prove or disprove whether your hypothesis is correct. Here is one possible hypothesis for this experiment: "A gentle flow of water across a downward sloping landscape will create a meandering stream path, while a more forceful flow will create a straighter path."

In this case, the **variable** you will change is the velocity of the water flow, and the variable you will measure is the resulting stream pattern. You expect the stream to meander for low flows and be straighter for higher flows.

Level of Difficulty

Easy.

How to Experiment Safely

Handle the bricks carefully to prevent injury.

Materials Needed

- flat outdoor area
- hose and water supply
- 24-inch (61-centimeter) long shallow pan, such as a plant tray
- 5 pounds (2.2 kilograms) sand for a sandbox
- 5 pounds (2.2 kilograms) gravel
- 2 bricks or wooden blocks for support

Approximate Budget

$8 for sand and gravel.

Timetable

45 minutes.

Step-by-Step Instructions

1. Pour equal amounts of gravel and sand into the tray and mix well. Make the surface level and smooth from one end to the other.

Steps 1 to 3: Set-up of sand and gravel tray.

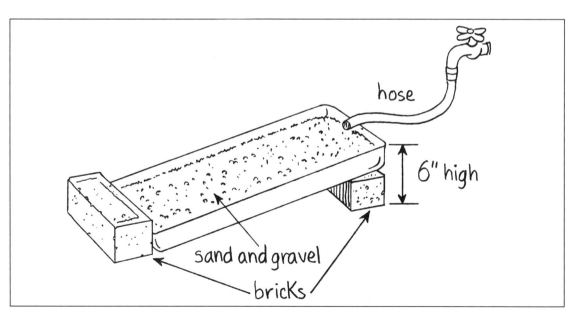

hose

6" high

sand and gravel

bricks

experiment
CENTRAL

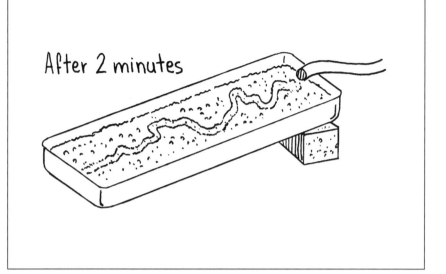

Step 6: Diagram the pattern of water flow after 4 minutes.

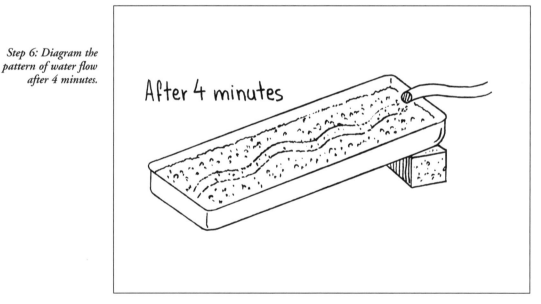

2. Lift one end approximately 6 inches (15 centimeters) high and place a brick underneath. Place the other brick in front of the lower end to keep it from sliding.

3. Place the end of the hose at the high end of the box.

4. Turn the hose on for 2 minutes, allowing a very soft flow of water to run over the sand.

Troubleshooter's Guide

Here is a problem that may arise during this experiment, a possible cause, and a way to remedy the problem.

Problem: The sand or gravel did not move or show a pattern in the first 2 minutes.

Possible cause: Not enough water was applied. Allow the water to flow longer, until a stream bank begins to form.

5. After 2 minutes, turn off the water and diagram the pattern of water.

6. Turn the water on again for 2 more minutes; then turn it off and diagram the pattern again.

7. Smooth the surface of the sand and gravel and repeat steps 4 through 6 with a higher water flow rate.

Summary of Results

Study your diagrams and the tray of sand. Which size particle of sand or gravel moved the most? As the stream flowed longer, how were the patterns affected? Did your stream begin to meander at the lower flowrate and go straighter at the higher flowrate? Write a paragraph summarizing your results and explaining them.

Change the Variables

To vary this experiment, experiment with the angle of the slope or the size of the particles in the streambed.

Design Your Own Experiment

How to Select a Topic Relating to this Concept

Rivers of water have carved Earth's landscape, whether flowing in streams and rivers or creeping slowly as glaciers. You can try other experiments relating to rivers, involving topics such as water velocity and turbidity (amount of mud in the water) or a river's rates of erosion, deposition, and weathering. You might also investigate underground rivers or cave-forming rivers.

Check the For More Information section and talk with your science teacher or school or communmity media specialist to start gathering information on river questions that interest you.

Steps in the Scientific Method

To do an original experiment, you need to plan carefully and think things through. Otherwise, you might not be sure what question you are answering, what you are or should be measuring, or what your findings prove or disprove.

Here are the steps in designing an experiment:

- State the purpose of—and the underlying question behind—the experiment you propose to do.
- Recognize the variables involved, and select one that will help you answer the question at hand.
- State a testable hypothesis, an educated guess about the answer to your question.
- Decide how to change the variable you selected.
- Decide how to measure your results.

Recording Data and Summarizing the Results

It is important that your data be kept organized in graphs or charts. When you finish your experiment, you must summarize the data and record your results. Reflect on the original question you wanted to answer. Write a paragraph explaining what happened and why so others can learn from your research.

Related Projects

To develop an experiment on this topic, think about a question that you want answered. Where does the water flow the fastest? What is the largest size rock that can be carried by a river? Where does the water come from and go to? Investigate ways to measure and analyze rivers in order to answer your questions.

For More Information

Knapp, Brian. *River.* Danbury, CT: Grolier Educational Corp., 1993. ❖ Offers facts about rivers, including how they work and rivers of the world. Includes simple experiments.

experiment
CENTRAL

Pringle, Lawrence. *Rivers and Lakes.* New York: Time-Life Books, 1985. ❖ Explains how rivers change the landscape and how their energy is harnessed. Good chapter about organisms and wildlife that depend on rivers for their survival.

chapter 48

Water Cycle

Water is found not only in oceans, rivers, streams, ponds, swamps, puddles, and similar places. It is also stored in the soil, in polar ice caps, and in underground areas called **aquifers.** Some water is actually in the air as **water vapor.** The **water cycle,** sometimes called the **hydrologic cycle,** is the continuous movement of water between the atmosphere, land, and bodies of water. Rainstorms are the major way that water gets from the atmosphere to Earth. Then the rain seeps into the soil or runs over land into streams, rivers, and oceans.

Over time, water evaporates from lakes, ponds, swamps, rivers, oceans, and even soil, changing from a liquid to a gas called water vapor. This water vapor rises into the atmosphere again, where it cools and **condenses** around dust or salt particles in the air, turning back into droplets of liquid. When the droplets get too heavy to remain in the air, they fall as **precipitation:** rain, snow, sleet, or hail.

Water vapor is often invisible, but on a warm summer day, you can feel water vapor. The air often feels damp because it contains a lot of water vapor.

How much water can the air hold?

There is a limit to how much water vapor air can hold. When the air becomes **saturated** with water vapor, the excess water vapor condenses into droplets of water. Water vapor high in the atmosphere forms clouds, large masses of droplets. When these clouds are close to the ground, we call them fog. You have probably also seen water vapor condense on windows or on cold drink glasses.

Words to Know

Aquifer:
Underground layer of sand, gravel, or spongy rock that collects water.

Condense/condensation:
The process by which a gas changes into a liquid.

Control experiment:
A set-up that is identical to the experiment but is not affected by the variable that affects the experimental group. Results from the control experiment are compared to results from the actual experiment.

Evaporate/evaporation:
The process by which liquid changes into a gas.

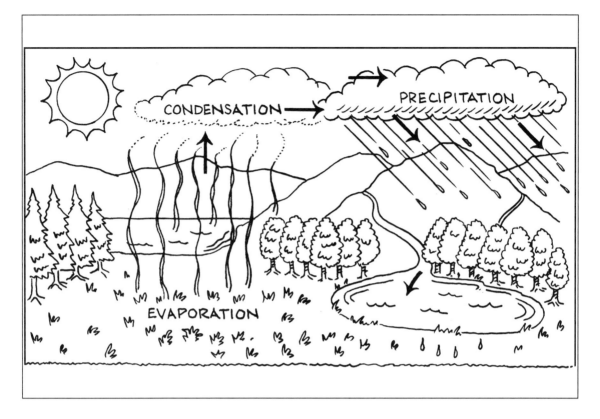

Illustration of global water cycle.

Is the water cycle a new idea?

The water cycle is driven by the Sun and gravity and affects climate, soils, erosion, habitat, transportation, and so on. This cycle has been recognized and studied by scientists for thousands of years. Leonardo da Vinci wrote about it in the 1400s. The founders of modern hydrologic study were Pierre Perroult (1608–1680), Edme Mariotte (1620–1684), and Edmund Halley (1656–1742). Today, people who study the water cycle are called **hydrologists.**

People can affect the water cycle. For example, paving land with concrete decreases the amount of water that can enter the soil. Using dams to create artificial lakes or reservoirs increases evaporation. What other factors affect the water cycle? How do temperature and surface area affect the rate at which water changes into water vapor? You will have an opportunity to explore these questions in the following two experiments.

Experiment 1
Temperature: How does temperature affect the rate of evaporation?

Purpose/Hypothesis

Evaporation occurs when liquid water turns into water vapor, a gas. The more water that evaporates and then condenses back into water droplets in the atmosphere, the more rain that falls.

In this experiment, you will determine how water temperature affects the rate of evaporation. Before you begin, make an educated guess about the outcome of this experiment based on your knowledge of evaporation. This educated guess, or prediction, is your **hypothesis**. A hypothesis should explain these things:

- the topic of the experiment
- the variable you will change
- the variable you will measure
- what you expect to happen

A hypothesis should be brief, specific, and measurable. It must be something you can test through observation. Your experiment will prove or disprove whether your hypothesis is correct. Here is one pos-

Precipitation:
Water in its liquid or frozen form when it falls from clouds in the atmosphere as rain, snow, sleet, or hail.

Saturated:
Containing the maximum amount of a solute for a given amount of solvent at a certain temperature.

Surface area:
The area of a body of water that is exposed to the air.

Variable:
Something that can affect the results of an experiment.

Water (hydrologic) cycle:
The constant movement of water molecules on Earth as they rise into the atmosphere as water vapor, condense into droplets and fall to land or bodies of water, evaporate, and rise again.

Water vapor:
Water in its gaseous state.

The water cycle is important to all life forms because it brings water continuously to land and removes many impurities along the way. (Photo Researchers Inc. Reproduced by permission.)

sible hypothesis for this experiment: "The warmer the water temperature, the more evaporation will occur."

In this case, the **variable** you will change will be the temperature of the water, and the variable you will measure will be the amount of water left in your containers at the end of the experiment. You expect the container with the warmer water will have less water left because more has evaporated into the air.

Setting up a **control experiment** will help you isolate one variable. Only one variable will change between the control and your experimental containers, and that is the water temperature. The control container will remain at room temperature. You will make the water in the experimental containers cooler or warmer than room temperature.

You will record the amount of water you put into your containers and the amount of water left after the containers spend a day at different temperatures. If the container with the hotter water has less water left in it, your hypothesis is correct.

What Are the Variables?

Variables are anything that might affect the results of an experiment. Here are the main variables in this experiment:

- the temperature of the water
- the temperature of the surrounding air
- the amount of water in each container at the beginning and end of the experiment
- the surface area of the water
- the amount of humidity or water vapor in the air

In other words, the variables in this experiment are everything that might affect the rate of evaporation of the water. If you change more than one variable, you will not be able to tell which variable had the most effect on the evaporation.

Level of Difficulty

Easy.

Materials Needed

- 3 containers of the same size, shape, and material
- 6 cups (3 pints or 1.4 liter) water
- ice cubes
- an insulated container large enough to hold one of the three containers above (an ice chest would work)
- thermometer
- measuring cup
- graduated cylinder
- flexible lamp

Approximate Budget

Less than $15. (Most of these materials should be available in the average household.)

Timetable

1 to 2 hours to set up and take the initial data, plus another 24 hours to take the final data.

Step-by-Step Instructions

TOP: Step 2: Set-up of three containers.

BOTTOM: Data sheet for Experiment 1.

1. Measure 2 cups (1 pint or 0.4 liters) of water into two containers. Fill the third container to the same level with a mixture of water and as many ice cubes as will fit. Mark the water level on the side of each container.

2. Label one container "control," the second one "warm," and the third one with the ice "cool."

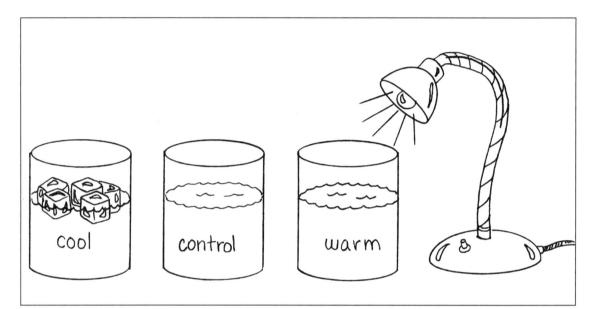

Jar	Air temperature	Water temperature	Amount of water left
cool			
control			
warm			

experiment
CENTRAL

How to Experiment Safely

If your containers are made of glass, handle them carefully. Also be careful not to touch the light bulb in the lamp.

3. Place all three containers in a room where the temperature is about 70 to 72°F (21 to 22°C). Use the thermometer to take the temperature, and record it on your data sheet.

4. Leave the control container as is. Place the cool container inside the insulated container. Take the water temperature and record it.

5. Place the flexible light so it shines directly on the warm container but does not warm the other two containers. After an hour or so, take the water temperature and record it.

6. Leave your containers in place for 24 hours.

7. The next day, use the graduated cylinder to measure the amount of water remaining in each container. Record your findings.

Summary of Results

Study your results. How did the air temperature affect the amount of evaporation from each container? Was your hypothesis correct? Summarize what you found.

Troubleshooter's Guide

Experiments do not always work out as planned. However, figuring out what went wrong can definitely be a learning experience. Here is a problem that may arise during this experiment, a possible cause, and ways to remedy the problem.

Problem: The containers all lost about the same amount of water.

Possible cause: The water temperatures were not different enough. Use more ice in the cool one, and place the light bulb closer to the warm one.

experiment

Change the Variables

You can change the variables and repeat this experiment to learn more. Try controlling the temperature more closely so you can measure the change in evaporation rate that occurs with a smaller temperature difference. You can also see if any changes in the results occur when you change the size or shape of your containers. What do you notice?

Experiment 2
Surface Area: How does surface area affect the rate of evaporation?

Purpose/Hypothesis

In this experiment, you will fill containers of different sizes with the same amount of water to explore how their **surface area** affects the rate of evaporation. For example, if you poured a certain amount of water in a tall, thin test tube with a small surface area, and the same amount in a short, broad cake pan with a large surface area, which container would have the greater rate of evaporation?

What Are the Variables?

Variables are anything that might affect the results of an experiment. Here are the main variables in this experiment:

• surface area of the water

• amount of water

• length of the experiment

• temperature of the water

• the temperature of the surrounding air

• the amount of humidity or water vapor in the air

In other words, the variables in this experiment are everything that might affect the rate of evaporation of the water. If you change more than one variable, you will not be able to tell which variable had the most effect on the evaporation.

Before you begin, make an educated guess about the outcome of this experiment based on your knowledge of evaporation. This educated guess, or prediction, is your **hypothesis**. A hypothesis should explain these things:

- the topic of the experiment
- the variable you will change
- the variable you will measure
- what you expect to happen

Which body of water do you think experiences the most evaporation? (Peter Arnold Inc. Reproduced by permission.)

A hypothesis should be brief, specific, and measurable. It must be something you can test through observation. Your experiment will prove or disprove whether your hypothesis is correct. Here is one possible hypothesis for this experiment: "A greater surface area will lead to faster evaporation."

In this case, the **variable** you will change will be the surface area of your trays. The variable you will measure is amount of evaporation that occurs.

For the **control experiment,** you will use a medium-sized tray. For the experimental containers, you will use larger and smaller trays. You will measure how much evaporation occurs by monitoring the water level in the trays over time and measuring the amount of water left. If the tray with the largest surface area shows the fastest rate of evaporation, then your hypothesis is correct.

Level of Difficulty
Easy.

Materials Needed
- 3 metal or plastic square or rectangular watertight trays or containers of different sizes
- ruler or tape measure
- water
- graduated cylinder

Approximate Budget
Less than $5. (Most of these materials should be available in the average household; try to borrow the graduated cylinder.)

Timetable
About 5 days.

How to Experiment Safely
There are no safety hazards in this experiment.

Step-by-Step Instructions

1. With your ruler, measure both sides of each tray. Multiply the two sides together to get the surface area of the tray. Record these numbers on your data sheet (see page 740).

2. Measure exactly the same volume of water into each tray. The amount is not important, as long as you know how much it is and put the same amount in each tray.

TOP: Step 1: Figuring the surface area of the tray.

BOTTOM: Steps 2 and 3: Set-up of the three trays. Place the trays side by side under the same conditions.

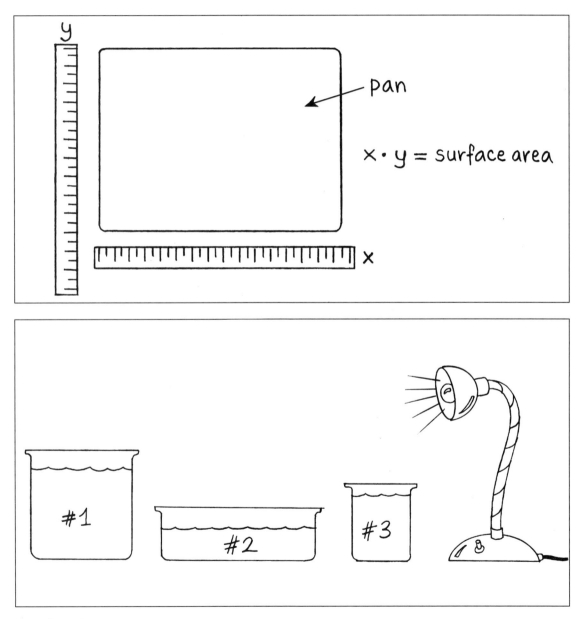

	Pan #	Surface area	Water left
Day #1			
Day #2			
Day #3			
Day #4			
Day #5			

Data sheet for Experiment 2.

3. Place the trays side by side under the same conditions. They should either all be exposed to sunlight or all be in the dark, for example.

4. After the trays sit for a day, pour the water from each tray into the graduated cylinder and measure it. Record this information on your data sheet, and pour the water back into the same tray. Be careful not to lose any water as you pour.

5. Repeat Step 4 every day for 5 days.

Summary of Results

To find out how much water evaporated each day, subtract the amount of water left each day from the amount from the previous day. Compare your findings. What have you discovered? Did the tray with the largest surface area lose the most water to evaporation? Did the tray with the smallest surface area lose water to evaporation at the slowest rate? Was your hypothesis correct? Summarize what you have found.

Change the Variables

You can vary this experiment in several ways. For example, you can use pans that are really big and really small. Compare the evaporation rates. What does this tell you about evaporation from lakes, ponds, and oceans?

experiment
CENTRAL

You can also experiment with the effect of temperature. Try moving all your pans to a very warm or very cool place, such as a refrigerator. What happens then? Be sure to record the temperature in the places you put the pans.

Finally, you can use containers with similar surface area but different depths. Determine the effect of depth on the evaporation rate.

Design Your Own Experiment

How to Select a Topic Relating to this Concept

If you are interested in the water cycle, you could study the evaporation rate when water is moving and still, investigate the evaporation differences between saltwater and fresh water, or compare how concrete and soil affect the rate of evaporation.

If you are more interested in condensation, you could try making your own clouds and studying the effects of water temperature, air temperature, and sizes of water bodies. Or you may want to study the surfaces on which rain falls on and measure how long it takes to evaporate or seep into the soil.

experiment
CENTRAL

Check the For More Information section and talk with your science teacher or school or community media specialist to start gathering information on water cycle questions that interest you.

Steps in the Scientific Method

To do an original experiment, you need to plan carefully and think things through. Otherwise you might not be sure what question you are answering, what your are or should be measuring, or what your findings prove or disprove.

Here are the steps in designing an experiment:

- State the purpose of—and underlying question behind—the experiment you propose to do.
- Recognize the variables involved, and select one that will help you answer the question at hand.
- State a testable hypothesis, an educated guess about the answer to your question.
- Decide how to change the variables you selected.
- Decide how to measure your results.

Recording Data and Summarizing the Results

Your data should include charts, such as the one you did for these experiments. They should be clearly labeled and easy to read. You may also want to include photos, graphs, or drawings of your experimental setup and results.

If you are preparing an exhibit, draw diagrams of your procedure and display your containers. If you have done a nonexperimental project, explain clearly what your research question was and illustrate your findings.

Related Projects

In addition to completing experiments, you could prepare models that demonstrate the water cycle or you could research how the water cycle is being affected by human actions, globally or locally. You might study the amounts of rainfall in different parts of the country and how landforms affect rainfall. You might go in many directions with your interests.

For More Information

Hooper, Meredith, and Christopher Coady. *The Drop in My Drink: The Story of*

Water on Our Planet. New York: Viking Children's Books, 1998. ❖ Detailed information on the water cycle, interesting facts about water, and important environmental information.

Walker, Sally M. *Water Up, Water Down: The Hydrologic Cycle.* Minneapolis, MN: Carolrhoda Earth Watch Book, 1992. ❖ Descriptions of the water cycle, historically important experiments, and the water cycle's importance to all life on Earth.

chapter 49

Weather

What is the weather like where you are today? **Weather** is the state of the troposphere at a particular time and place. The **troposphere** is the lowest layer of Earth's atmosphere, ranging to an altitude of about 9 miles (15 kilometers) above Earth's surface.

How is weather different from climate?

Climate is the average weather that a region experiences over a long period. A change in the weather can mean a rain shower. A change in climate might consist of a year-round warming trend that affects how crops grow in a region.

All weather starts with the Sun's heat, but the Sun does not heat Earth's surface evenly. The Sun's direct rays make the equator regions much warmer than other areas, while the tilt of Earth's axis causes the hemisphere that is tilted toward the Sun to be warmer than the hemisphere that is tilted away from the Sun.

The elements of weather include temperature, **humidity**, cloudiness, precipitation (rain, snow, hail), wind, and air pressure. These elements interact to spread the Sun's heat more evenly around the Earth. Without them, the equator region would get much hotter than it does, while the pole regions would get colder.

What causes wind?

Air moves because of differences in both temperature and air pressure, also called atmospheric pressure. **Atmospheric pressure** is the pressure exerted by the atmosphere at Earth's surface due to the weight of the air.

Ⓦords to Know

Anemometer:
A device that measures wind speed.

Atmospheric pressure:
The pressure exerted by the atmosphere at Earth's surface due to the weight of the air.

Climate:
The average weather that a region experiences over a long period.

Control experiment:
A set-up that is identical to the experiment but is not affected by the variable that will be changed during the experiment.

experiment
CENTRAL

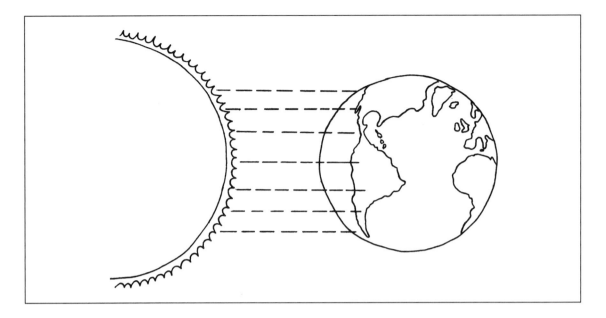

As the Sun heats Earth's surface, the surface heats the air above it. As the air molecules warm up, they move farther apart. This reduces the **density** or heaviness of the air and creates an area of low air pressure. On the other hand, molecules in cool air are closer together, making that air denser and heavier. Cool air creates an area of high air pressure.

Air moves from areas of high pressure to areas of low pressure, creating wind. During Project 1, you will build an **anemometer** (pronounced an-eh-MOM-eter), a device that measures the speed of wind.

What causes clouds?

As warm air rises into the atmosphere, it carries with it **water vapor,** which is water in its gas form. As the air cools, the gas molecules move closer together and condense around very small particles of dust or salt in the air. The water vapor turns into its liquid form, water droplets. Clouds are huge masses of condensed water vapor.

As the droplets bump into each other, they join to form larger drops. In time, they are large and heavy enough to fall as rain. One rain drop can contain a million cloud droplets!

An English naturalist named Luke Howard gave cloud groups these Latin names in 1803:

- Cirrus (pronounced SEAR-us, from the Latin word for "curl of hair")
- Stratus (from the Latin word for "layer")

Words to Know

Density: The mass of a substance compared to its volume.

Ecosystem:
An ecological community, including plants, animals, and microorganisms, considered together with their environment.

Hypothesis:
An idea in the form of a statement that can be tested by observation and/or experiment.

experiment
CENTRAL

- Cumulus (pronounced CUME-u-lus, from the Latin word for "heap")
- Nimbus (from the Latin word for "rain")

As warm, light air rises, cooler, heavier air rushes in to take its place. (Photo Researchers Inc. Reproduced by permission.)

Since then, **meteorologists** have used Howard's names to describe ten types of clouds at three levels.

High-level clouds about 20,000 feet (6.0 kilometers) above Earth include Cirrus, wispy clouds that precede bad weather; Cirrostratus, layers of clouds that signal rain; and Cirrocumulus, rippled clouds that signal unsettled weather

Middle-level clouds about 7,000 to 17,000 feet (2.1 to 5.2 kilometers) above Earth include Altocumulus, flat gray-white clouds that precede a summer storm; Altostratus, layers of gray clouds that indicate it will rain soon; and Nimbostratus, thick dark-gray clouds that signal rain or snow.

experiment
CENTRAL

Recognizing different types of clouds can help you predict the weather. (Photo Researchers Inc. Reproduced by permission.)

Low-level clouds less than 7,000 feet (2.1 kilometers) above Earth include Stratocumulus, gray or white rolls that indicate dry weather; Stratus, layers of gray clouds that often bring precipitation; Cumulus, fluffy white puffs seen on hot summer days; and Cumulonimbus, dark, towering clouds that bring storms.

Weather affects what we wear, what we eat, the kinds of work we do, how we have fun, and, most importantly, the **ecosystem** in which we live. Learning more about the weather helps us better understand the world in which we live.

Words to Know

Troposphere:
The lowest layer of Earth's atmosphere, ranging to an altitude of about 9 miles (15 kilometers) above Earth's surface.

Variable:
Something that can affect the results of an experiment.

Project 1
Wind: Measuring wind speed with a homemade anemometer

Purpose

In this project, you will make a simple anemometer and compare the wind speed measured by your anemometer with the wind speed measured in your region by the National Weather Service. The National Weather Service gathers wind speed and other weather information every 1 to 6 hours from about 1,000 land stations throughout the United States and its possessions. Meteorologists at the Weather Service use this information to make weather predictions, which are then broadcast over radio and television. The Service's weather stations use cup anemometers to measure wind speed.

This cup anemometer is connected to instruments inside the weather station that record how many times the cups spin in a certain period of time. The spinning rate indicates the wind speed. (Photo Researchers Inc. Reproduced by permission.)

Some television stations provide a live broadcast of the current wind speed; you might even see the speed change during the forecast. If you can tune in to one of these broadcasts, you can make your wind speed measurements simultaneously, thus eliminating the time variable.

Level of Difficulty
Easy/moderate.

Materials Needed
- metal or plastic protractor
- Ping-Pong ball
- 8 inches (20 centimeters) of strong thread
- transparent tape

Approximate Budget
Less than $5. (Most or all of these materials should be available in the average household.)

Timetable
15 to 20 minutes.

Words to Know

Water vapor:
Water in its gas form.

Weather:
The state of the troposphere at a particular time and place.

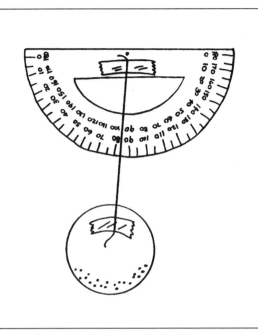

Steps 1 and 2: Set-up of Ping-Pong ball and protractor.

Step-by-Step Instructions

1. Tape one end of the thread firmly to the Ping-Pong ball.

2. Tie the other end of the thread to the middle of the flat side of the protractor, as illustrated. The ball should hang down so the thread crosses the rounded side of the protractor. The numbers (angles) marked on the rounded side will indicate wind speed.

Step 6: Data chart for Project 1.

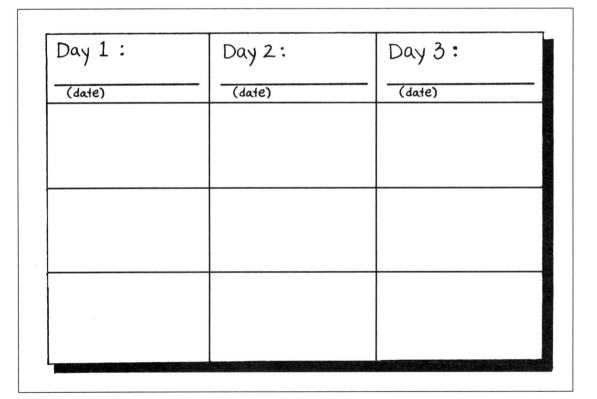

Day 1 : _____	Day 2 : _____	Day 3 : _____
(date)	(date)	(date)

3. Determine when the weather will be broadcast over a local radio or television station and whether it includes a live broadcast of wind speed.

4. At the same time as a live weather broadcast or about 2 hours before a taped broadcast, take your anemometer outside. Stand in an open area, away from trees, buildings, and traffic.

5. Hold the anemometer by one corner, with the flat side parallel to the ground.

6. As the wind blows, note the angle of the farthest movement of the thread. Record it on a chart similar to the one illustrated.

7. Use the scale provided to convert the angle to miles per hour (mph) and record it on your chart:

Angle	Mph
90	0
80	15

Troubleshooter's Guide

Here is a problem that may arise during this project, some possible causes, and ways to remedy the problem.

Problem: Your wind speed reading was much higher or lower than the one broadcast on radio or television.

Possible causes:

1. You took your reading in a spot that is protected from the wind or a spot that serves as a natural wind tunnel, increasing its speed and force. Try again in a different spot.

2. You took your reading at a different time from the reading that was broadcast. Try calling the radio or television station and see if the forecaster or someone else will give you the current wind speed. Then quickly do your own reading.

Angle	Mph
70	20
60	25
50	30
40	35
30	40
20	50

8. Take a second wind-speed measurement and record it on the chart.

9. Add the wind speed from the radio or television broadcast to your chart.

10. Repeat Steps 4 to 9 on two more days and record the results.

Summary of Results

Use the data on your chart to create a triple-bar graph comparing the three readings on each day. Then study your graph and chart and how accurately your anemometer measured wind speed. Were your own measurements on any day within 5 miles per hour (8 kilometers per hour) of those given in the radio or television broadcast? Write a paragraph summarizing your findings.

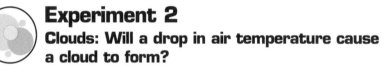

Experiment 2
Clouds: Will a drop in air temperature cause a cloud to form?

Purpose/Hypothesis

In this experiment, you will create a cloud in a bottle by making water vapor condense around tiny smoke particles in the air. To make the vapor condense, you will suddenly reduce the air pressure, allowing the water vapor molecules to move farther apart and cool off.

But is it the drop in temperature that causes the cloud to form? And will a cloud form without tiny particles in the air? To find out, you will also try the experiment without a drop in temperature and without smoke particles in the air. (You might need a helper to complete these experiments.)

Before you begin, make an educated guess about the outcome of this experiment based on your knowledge of clouds. This educated

experiment
CENTRAL

guess, or prediction, is your **hypothesis.** A hypothesis should explain these things:

- the topic of the experiment
- the variable you will change
- the variable you will measure
- what you expect to happen

A hypothesis should be brief, specific, and measurable. It must be something you can test through observation. Here is one possible hypothesis for this experiment: "A cloud will form only after a drop in temperature and only when particles are present in the air."

In this case, the **variable** you will change in the first part of the experiment is the air pressure (and hence the air temperature), and the variable you will change in the second part of the experiment is the presence of smoke particles in the bottle. The variable you will measure in both parts of the experiment is the presence of a cloud. You expect the cloud will form only when the temperature drops and particles are present.

What Are the Variables?

Variables are anything that might affect the results of an experiment. Here are the main variables in this experiment:

- how much the air pressure increases and then drops inside the bottle

- whether the bottle contains smoke particles and how many particles are present

- whether the bottle is tightly sealed

- the amount of water in the bottom of the bottle

- the air temperature outside the bottle

   In other words, the variables in this experiment are everything that might affect the formation of a cloud. If you change more than one variable, you will not be able to tell which variable had the most effect on the cloud formation.

You will complete two **control experiments.** In one, you will determine whether a cloud will form without a drop in temperature. In the other control experiment, you will see if a cloud will form without smoke particles in the air. If a cloud forms only when the temperature drops and when particles are present, you will know that your hypothesis is correct.

Level of Difficulty
Easy/moderate—but you may need someone to help you manipulate the materials.

Materials Needed
- three 1-quart (1-liter) plastic soda bottles, empty and clean, with caps
- matches
- flashlight
- labels and a marker
- measuring cup
- water

Approximate Budget
Less than $5. (Most materials should be available in the average household.)

Timetable
1 hour.

Step-by-Step Instructions
1. Label one bottle "Experimental" and two bottles "Control."

2. Pour 1 cup of water into each bottle.

3. Drop two lighted matches into the Experimental bottle and quickly screw on the cap.

4. Let the matches burn until the water puts them out.

5. Shake the bottle to make the air inside moist.

6. With the bottle upright, squeeze the bottle to increase the air pressure inside.

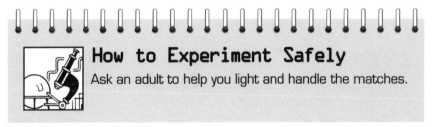

How to Experiment Safely
Ask an adult to help you light and handle the matches.

experiment
CENTRAL

cap screwed
on tightly

smoke

water

Experimental Bottle:	Results Observed:
Experimental Bottle:	Results Observed:
Experimental Bottle:	Results Observed:

7. Place the flashlight so it shines into the bottle (or have your helper hold the flashlight).

8. Quickly unscrew the cap to lower the pressure inside the bottle and cool off the water vapor.

9. Check to see if a cloud forms. If it does, it will last only a few seconds. Record your observations on a chart similar to the one illustrated.

TOP: Steps 3 to 7: Set-up of cloud experiment.

BOTTOM: Step 9: Data chart for Experiment 2.

10. Using one of the Control bottles, repeat Steps 3 through 9, omitting Step 8. (Do not unscrew the cap, so the air pressure and temperature of the water vapor inside the bottle do not change.)

11. Observe this Control bottle for at least 3 minutes to see whether a cloud forms. Record your observations.

12. Using the other Control bottle, repeat Steps 5 through 9. (This time, you do not perform Steps 3 and 4 so the bottle contains no smoke particles.)

13. Observe the second Control bottle for at least 3 minutes to see whether a cloud forms. Record your observations.

 ## Troubleshooter's Guide

Here are some problems that may arise during this experiment, some possible causes, and ways to remedy the problems.

Problem: A cloud did not seem to form inside the Experimental bottle.

Possible causes:

1. The air pressure did not get high enough inside the bottle. Try again, squeezing the bottle harder.

2. You unscrewed the cap too slowly, allowing the air to cool so slowly that the water vapor did not condense. Try again, unscrewing it as quickly as possible.

3. The bottle did not contain enough smoke particles. Try again, dropping in three or four lighted matches.

4. You did not look into the bottle quickly enough and missed the cloud. Try again, and have a helper unscrew the cap so you can observe what is happening.

Problem: A cloud formed in the Control bottle that contained no smoke particles.

Possible cause: The air in the bottle already contained other tiny particles. Rinse the bottle and try again.

Summary of Results

Study the findings on your chart and decide whether your hypothesis was correct. In which bottles did a cloud form? Write a paragraph summarizing your findings and explaining whether they support your hypothesis.

Change the Variables

Here are some ways you can vary this experiment:

- Try increasing or reducing the amount of smoke particles, or try adding dust to the air inside the bottle instead of smoke particles.
- Experiment with the amount of water in the bottle. Try the experiment with no water at all.
- Complete the experiment using saltwater and no smoke particles. Shake the bottle vigorously to release salt from the water into the air. (Most cloud particles actually form around salt released into the air from ocean waves.)
- Try doing the experiment outside on a chilly day. Instead of unscrewing the cap, see if the air outside the bottle chills the air inside enough to form a cloud.

Design Your Own Experiment

How to Select a Topic Relating to this Concept

You can explore many other aspects of weather. Consider what you would like to know about this topic. For example, you might want to find out how Earth's rotation affects wind direction. Or you might try your hand at predicting the weather by observing clouds.

Check the For More Information section and talk with your science teacher or school or community media specialist to start gathering information on weather questions that interest you. As you consider possible experiments, be sure to discuss them with your science teacher or another knowledgeable adult before trying them. Some of the materials or procedures might be dangerous.

Steps in the Scientific Method

To do an original experiment, you need to plan carefully and think things through. Otherwise, you might not be sure which question you are answering, what you are or should be measuring, or what your findings prove or disprove.

Here are the steps in designing an experiment:

- State the purpose of—and the underlying question behind—the experiment you propose to do.
- Recognize the variables involved, and select one that will help you answer the question at hand.
- State a testable hypothesis, an educated guess about the answer to your question.
- Decide how to change the variable you selected.
- Decide how to measure your results.

Recording Data and Summarizing the Results

In your wind speed and cloud-making experiments, your raw data might include charts, graphs, drawings, and photographs of the changes you observed. If you display your experiment, make clear the question you are trying to answer, the variable you changed, the variable you measured, the results, and your conclusions. Explain what materials you used, how long each step took, and other basic information.

Related Projects

You can undertake a variety of projects related to weather. For example, you might find out how seeding clouds produces rain. Or you could try an experiment with a pan of flour that will show you the different sizes of raindrops. Now that you have an anemometer, you might make a weather vane to determine wind direction, a rain gauge to keep track of rainfall, and a hydrometer to measure the humidity in the air.

For More Information

Baker, Thomas. *Two Suns and a Green Sky: 22 Out-of-This-World Weather Models and Experiments*. New York: TAB Books, 1994. ❖ Offers clear instructions on setting up weather models and experiments.

Gardner, Robert, and David Webster. *Science Projects about Weather*. Hillside, NJ: Enslow Publishers, 1994. ❖ Describes science projects focusing on all aspects of weather and includes instructions on making weather forecasting devices.

Kerrod, Robin. *The Weather*. New York: Marshall Cavendish, 1994. ❖ Explains why and how air moves, how moisture affects the weather, and how climates are created.

Van Cleave, Janice. *201 Awesome, Magical, Bizarre, & Incredible Experiments*. New York: Wiley, 1994. ❖ Outlines experiments in earth science, astronomy, biology, chemistry, and physics, including a number of projects related to weather.

Van Cleave, Janice. *Weather*. New York: Wiley, 1995. ❖ Presents facts and experiments relating to weather.

chapter 50

Weather Forecasting

Weather forecasting, the scientific prediction of weather patterns, may look simple when we watch a television weather forecast on the local news, but it's not. That forecast was based on data collected and analyzed from many sources.

Weather sleuths everywhere

About 12,000 weather stations throughout the world communicate weather observations and data to international weather centers every three hours where the information is analyzed by **meteorologists,** who study the weather and the atmosphere. The weather stations consist of outdoor shelters, known as Stevenson screens, that house instruments such as thermometers, which measure air temperature, and anemometers, which record wind speed. All instruments at these stations are of the same type and accuracy.

Weather stations also record many other weather elements, including types of clouds, humidity, air pressure, precipitation (rainfall or snowfall), and visibility. Instruments and equipment that record weather in the upper atmosphere include radar, satellites, **radiosonde balloons,** and planes. Radar tracks the path of storms, while satellites send back pictures of entire weather systems. The radiosonde balloons carry instruments that record weather conditions in the upper atmosphere and send the data back by radio. Planes with special meteorological equipment track storms and their weather patterns.

A supercomputer collects all this information, calculates how air pressure, moisture, and winds might affect each other, and produces a forecast for the next 24 hours.

Words to Know

Barometer:
A device that measures air pressure.

Condensation:
The process by which a gas changes into a liquid.

Control experiment:
A set-up that is identical to the experiment but is not affected by the variable that will be changed during the experiment.

Dewpoint:
The point at which water vapor begins to condense.

Front:
The front edges of moving masses of air.

experiment
CENTRAL

Anemometers record wind speed. (Photo Researchers Inc. Reproduced by permission.)

Words to Know

High air pressure:
An area where the air is cooler and more dense, and the air pressure is higher than normal.

Hypothesis:
An idea in the form of a statement that can be tested by observation and/or experiment.

Isobars:
Continuous lines that connect areas with the same air pressure.

Low air pressure:
An area where the air is warmer and less dense, and the air pressure is lower than normal.

Meteorologist:
Scientist who studies the weather and the atmosphere.

Radiosonde balloons:
Instruments for collecting data in the atmosphere and then transmitting that data back to Earth by means of radio waves.

experiment
CENTRAL

Weather forecasting before computers

The first weather forecasting guide was written about 2,000 years ago. A Greek naturalist named Theophrastus wrote the *Book of Signs,* a collection of 200 natural signs that indicated the type of weather that was on its way. In 1687, John Tulley of Saybrook, Connecticut, published a farmers' almanac that included the first weather forecast made in the United States. In 1792, Robert Bailey Thomas of West Boyleston, Massachusetts, began writing an annual almanac, which

Satellites can track deadly hurricanes and alert those people who live in their path. (Photo Researchers Inc. Reproduced by permission.)

he eventually called *The Old Farmer's Almanac.* Along with humorous stories, Thomas offered some of the nation's earliest long-range weather forecasts.

Instruments such as the weathervane, which indicates wind direction, were used at least 2,000 years ago in Athens, Greece. In the seventeenth century, more precise weather instruments emerged that could indicate humidity, temperature, and barometric pressure, as well as wind direction and rainfall. The real science of **meteorology** (pronounced ME-tee-or-ology), the study of the atmosphere and weather, began during this era.

Measuring the air's ups and downs

One of the most important meteorological instruments was the **barometer,** which measures air pressure changes with a column of mercury that rises and falls. Air pressure differences between two adjoining areas of the atmosphere cause winds, and the barometer made it possible to predict wind velocity patterns. Many people worked on the design and theory of the barometer, but Evangelista Torricelli of Italy (1608–47) is generally credited with developing the first one in 1644.

Weather maps and computers

Weather maps have **isobars,** continuous lines that connect areas with the same air pressure. Meteorologists use isobars to observe the development of high and low pressure areas. A **high pressure area** is surrounded by winds that blow clockwise in the northern hemisphere and counterclockwise in the southern hemisphere. It usually brings dry weather. A **low pressure area** is surrounded by winds that blow counterclockwise in the northern hemisphere and clockwise in the southern hemisphere. It usually brings cloudy, wet, and windy weather.

Meteorologists also study the formation and movements of **fronts,** the front edges of moving masses of air. When cold air lies behind the edge, it is known as a cold front. When warm air lies behind, it is a warm front.

Computer forecasting techniques were first developed in the 1950s. The computer evaluates current weather conditions in a large area and then predicts changes that will occur in the next 10 minutes. This generates a new set of weather conditions, and the predictions continue until the computer has created a forecast for the next day's

Tornado watches are post-ed for a region when weather conditions are likely to form these destructive storms. (The Stock Market. Reproduced by permission.)

experiment
CENTRAL

weather. With today's supercomputers, the several billion computations required for a single forecast can be worked out very quickly.

Warning people of hurricanes and tornadoes is an important function of weather forecasting. Understanding weather terms and the formation of storms can help you avoid surprises and stay safe. In the experiment that follows, you will learn more about why and when **condensation** forms. The project will enable you to build your own barometer to help you make your own weather forecasts.

Experiment 1
Dewpoint: When will dew form?

Purpose/Hypothesis
This experiment deals with a principle of weather called **dewpoint**. Dew is the moisture that forms on plants and other objects when air is cooled sufficiently for the water vapor in the air to condense into liquid. The temperature at which dew forms is called the dewpoint temperature. If

What Are the Variables?
Variables are anything that might affect the results of an experiment. Here are the main variables in this experiment:

- the amount of water vapor present in the atmosphere

- the current weather conditions, including air temperature

- how fast the thermometer is swung during the experiment

   In other words, the variables in this experiment are everything that might affect the dry bulb and wet bulb temperatures (and hence the dewpoint temperature). If you change more than one variable, you will not be able to tell which variable had the most effect on the dewpoint.

Dewpoint Temperatures

Dry Bulb Tempera-ture (°C)	Difference Between Wet-Bulb and Dry Bulb Temperatures (°C)														
	1	2	3	4	5	6	7	8	9	10	11	12	13	14	15
−20	−33														
−18	−28														
−16	−24														
−14	−21	−36													
−12	−18	−28													
−10	−14	−22													
−8	−12	−18	−29												
−6	−10	−14	−22												
−4	−7	−12	−17	−29											
−2	−5	−8	−13	−20											
0	−3	−6	−9	−15	−24										
2	−1	−3	−6	−11	−17										
4	1	−1	−4	−7	−11	−19									
6	4	1	−1	−4	−7	−13									
8	6	3	1	−2	−5	−9	−21	−14							
10	8	6	4	1	−2	−5	−14	−9	−28						
12	10	8	6	4	1	−2	−9	−5	−16						
14	12	11	9	6	4	1	−5	−1	−10	−17					
16	14	13	11	9	7	4	−2	2	−6	−10	−17				
18	16	15	13	11	9	7	1	4	−2	−5	−10	−19			
20	19	17	15	14	12	10	4	8	2	−2	−5	−10	−19		
22	21	19	17	16	14	12	7	10	5	3	−1	−5	−10	−19	
24	23	21	20	18	16	15	10	13	8	6	2	−1	−5	−10	−18
26	25	23	22	20	18	17	12	16	11	9	6	3	0	−4	−9
28	27	25	24	22	21	19	17	18	14	11	9	7	4	1	−3
30	29	27	26	24	23	21	18	19	16	14	12	10	8	5	1

Dewpoint temperature chart.

the dewpoint temperature is close to the air temperature, there is a high possibility of fog, rain, or snow during the next few hours.

In this experiment, you will first determine the dewpoint temperature for that day. Then you will use what you have learned to guess or predict whether dew will form on a cold glass left outdoors. Before you begin, make an educated guess about the outcome of this experiment based on your knowledge of weather. This educated guess, or prediction, is your **hypothesis.** A hypothesis should explain these things:

*   the topic of the experiment
*   the variable you will change
*   the variable you will measure
*   what you expect to happen

A hypothesis should be brief, specific, and measurable. It must be something you can test through observation. Your experiment will

experiment
CENTRAL

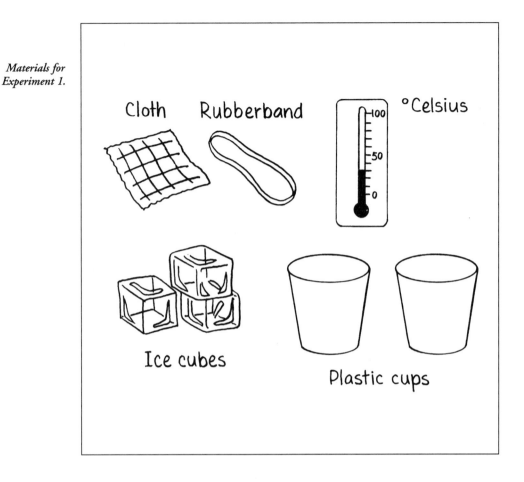

Cloth   Rubberband   °Celsius

Ice cubes   Plastic cups

prove or disprove your hypothesis. Here is one possible hypothesis for this experiment: " If the dewpoint temperature is close to 32°F (0°C), dew should develop on a glass of ice water."

In this case, the **variable** you will change is the temperature of the glass, and the variable you will measure is the formation of dew. You expect dew to form on the glass of ice water if the dewpoint temperature for that day is near freezing.

As a **control experiment**, you will set up one glass of water at air temperature. That way, you can determine whether dew forms no matter what the temperature of the glass. If dew forms only on the cold glass, your hypothesis will be supported.

Level of Difficulty

Easy.

Materials Needed

- thermometer (for safety, use an alcohol thermometer with red fluid inside)
- dewpoint temperature chart (illustrated on page 765)
- 1-inch (2.5-centimeter) square of cloth
- small rubber band
- water (at air temperature)
- ice
- 2 plastic or glass drinking cups (any size)

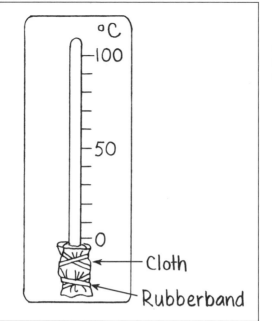

Step 2: Thermometer with cloth banded to the bottom. Wet cloth thoroughly.

Approximate Budget

About $10, if thermometers need to be purchased.

Timetable

30 minutes each day; experiment can be repeated each day for a week, if you wish.

Step-by-Step Instructions

1. Using the thermometer, take a reading of the outside air temperature and record it on a data sheet. This will be the "dry bulb temperature."

2. Place the cloth around the bulb at the bottom of the thermometer and wrap the rubber band around to hold the cloth securely. Wet the cloth thoroughly with tap water.

How to Experiment Safely

Always use caution when handling thermometers. If a thermometer should break, ask an adult for assistance in cleaning it up.

3. Wave the thermometer with the wet cloth in the air for 1 minute. Be sure to hold the thermometer at the top, at the opposite end of the cloth. Do not touch the thermometer stem.

4. Record the temperature shown on the thermometer. This will be the "wet bulb temperature."

5. On the data sheet, write the difference between the wet bulb and dry bulb temperatures. Example: Dry Bulb Temperature is 61°F (16°C). Wet Bulb Temperature is 50°F (10°C). The difference is 11°F (6°C).

6. Using the data you have collected, refer to the dewpoint temperature chart. Locate the dry bulb temperature in the left column. Locate the difference in wet and dry bulb temperatures across the top of the chart. Find where the two points intersect and record that number as the dewpoint temperature.

7. Fill one cup with water and ice cubes. The approximate temperature of the water will be 32°F (0°C). Fill the second cup (your control experiment) with water at normal tap water temperature.

8. Leave both cups outdoors in the shade for 30 minutes.

9. Check the outside of both cups for condensation. Record whether your hypothesis is correct. (The cup with ice water should always be below the dewpoint temperature and collect condensation. The cup at air temperature should remain dry unless the air temperature matches the dewpoint temperature.)

Troubleshooter's Guide

Here is a problem that may arise during this experiment, a possible cause, and a way to remedy the problem.

Problem: Condensation does not form on either glass.

Possible cause: The air does not contain enough water vapor. Place the cups in a different spot (outside or inside) or repeat the experiment on a different day.

Summary of Results

Create a chart to organize your results. If you repeat this experiment for several days, notice if dew has formed on the cup surfaces each morning. Replace the ice every day.

Change the Variables

You can vary this experiment in several ways. The air temperature and the amount of water vapor in the air change from day to day. If you change the locations or seasons in which you try this experiment, you can see different results. During spring and fall, high water vapor tends to be present. Indoor environments during the winter months often have less water vapor present.

Project 2
Air Pressure: How can air pressure be measured?

Purpose

Changes in the atmosphere are the cause of most of our weather. The purpose of this project is to build a barometer that shows changes in air pressure. When air is warmed, it rises and the air pressure decreases. If the air is cooled, it sinks and air pressure increases. Low air pressure usually indicates stormy weather, and high air pressure usually indicates fair weather. By observing air pressure trends, you will be able to predict upcoming weather conditions.

Level of Difficulty

Easy.

Materials Needed

- wide-mouth jar without a lid
- 7-inch (17.5-centimeter) diameter round balloon
- plastic straw
- index card
- rubber cement
- scissors

Approximate Budget

$1 for balloon.

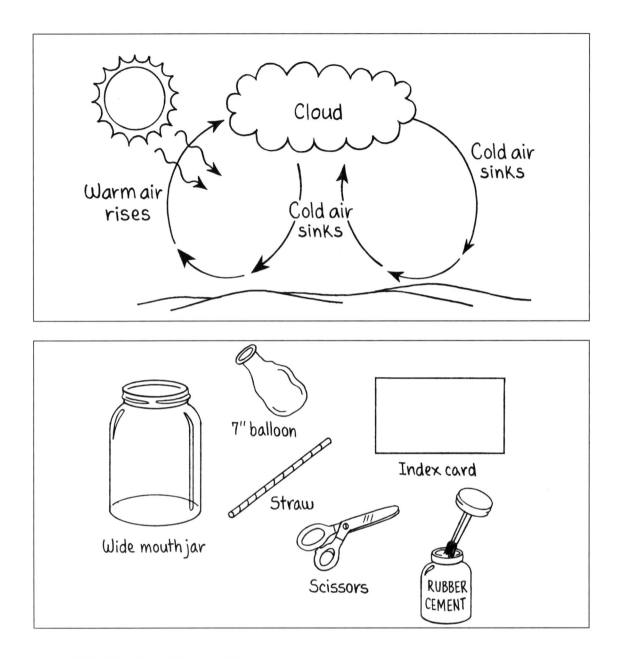

TOP: When air is warmed, it rises and the air pressure decreases. If the air is cooled, it sinks and air pressure increases.

BOTTOM: Materials for Project 2.

Timetable

20 minutes to prepare barometer; 1 to 2 weeks to observe changes in air pressure.

Step-by-Step Instructions

1. Cut end off the balloon and stretch the balloon over the mouth of the jar.

How to Work Safely

Use caution in handling the scissors.

2. Use the rubber band to attach the balloon securely to the jar.

3. Rubber cement the straw horizontally to the center of the balloon, so most of it extends over the edge of the jar.

4. Prop up the index card behind the straw. Line up the straw with the middle of the index card, but not touching it.

5. Draw a line behind the straw and label it "baseline."

6. Draw a line 0.5 inch (1 centimeter) above the baseline and label it "high pressure—fair weather."

7. Draw a line 0.5 inch (1 centimeter) below the baseline and label it "low pressure—poor weather."

8. Place the barometer outdoors in the shade and watch for changes in air pressure.

9. Record your observations along with daily weather conditions.

Illustration of completed barometer.

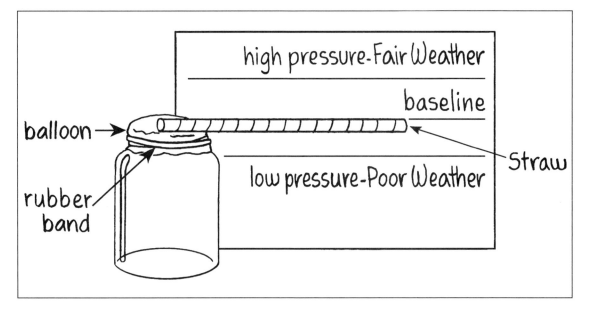

Troubleshooter's Guide

Here is a problem that may arise during this experiment, a possible cause, and a way to remedy the problem.

Problem: The straw on the balloon does not move.

Possible cause: If no change is noticeable, test the barometer by using a hair dryer to warm up the air in the jar. Adjust the balloon until the straw dips down.

Summary of Results

Can you explain changes in the readings on your barometer? (If the air pressure outside increases, it presses on the balloon and causes the straw to rise. If the air pressure outside drops below the pressure in the jar, the balloon swells, and the straw points downward.) For a fun experiment, try monitoring the environment inside your home. Leave the barometer in different rooms and record the results.

Design Your Own Experiment

How to Select a Topic Relating to this Concept

The day's weather conditions affect your daily routine and sometimes your mood. Since weather is always changing and is different around the globe, it presents many study possibilities. Possible weather topics include precipitation, humidity, air masses, hurricanes, tornadoes, and El Niño.

Check the For More Information section and talk with your science teacher or school or community media specialist to start gathering information on weather forecasting questions that interest you.

Steps in the Scientific Method

To do an original experiment, you need to plan carefully and think things through. Otherwise, you might not be sure what question your are answering, what you are or should be measuring, or what your findings prove or disprove.

Here are the steps in designing an experiment:

- State the purpose of—and the underlying question behind—the experiment you propose to do.
- Recognize the variables involved, and select one that will help you answer the question at hand.
- State a testable hypothesis, an educated guess about the answer to your question.
- Decide how to change the variable you selected.
- Decide how to measure your results.

Recording Data and Summarizing the Results

Experiments help us answer questions, so it is important to save your experiment results; keep a journal and jot notes and measurements in it. Your experiment can then be used by others and help answer their questions.

Related Projects

When thinking about experimenting in weather, focus on one specific field. For example, if you decide to examine similarities in weather between New York City, NY, and London, England, you might compare weather patterns. When you start exploring possible projects, you will be amazed at the range of experiments and projects available.

For More Information

Kerrod, Robin. *Young Scientist Concepts & Projects: Weather.* Milwaukee, WI: Garth Stevens Publishing, 1998. ❖ Offers a fact file and learn-it-yourself project book.

McVey, Vicki. *The Sierra Club Book of Weather Wisdom.* Boston: Little, Brown and Company, 1991. ❖ Includes dramatic weather stories from around the world, weather facts, and hands-on activities, games, and experiments.

Peacock, Graham. *Meteorology.* New York: Thompson Learning, 1995. ❖ Provides interesting information about weather and climate.

Taylor, Barbara. *Weather and Climate.* New York: Kingfisher Books, 1993. ❖ Outlines weather and geography facts and experiments.

budget index

Under $5

Bold type indicates volume number.

budget index

$5—$10

experiment
CENTRAL

Bold type indicates volume number.

budget index

experiment
CENTRAL

$21—$25

$26—$30

$31—$35

budget index

Bold type indicates volume number.

level of difficulty index

Easy

Easy means that the average student should easily be able to complete the tasks outlined in the project/experiment, and that the time spent on the project is not overly restrictive.

Bold type indicates volume number.

Moderate

Moderate means that the average student should find tasks outlined in the project/experiment challenging but not difficult, and that the time spent project/experiment may be more extensive.

Bold type indicates volume number.

level of
difficulty
index

Moderate/Difficult

Moderate/Difficult means that the average student should find tasks outlined in the project/experiment challenging, and that the time spent on the project/experiment may be more extensive.

Difficult

Difficult means that the average student will probably find the tasks outlined in the project/experiment mentally and physically challenging, and that the time spent on the project/experiment will be more extensive.

Bold type indicates volume number.

timetable index

Bold type indicates
volume number.

experiment
CENTRAL

2 hours

Bold type indicates volume number.

experiment
CENTRAL

3-4 weeks

2 months

4 months

Bold type indicates volume number.

timetable index

experiment
CENTRAL

general index

A

Abscission **1**: 92
Acceleration **2**: 278
Acid **1**: 1, 76, **3**: 477
Acid rain **1**: 1-18, **3**: 479, 480 [ill.]
Acoustics **4**: 591
Active solar energy system **4**: 576
Adhesion **4**: 697, 698 [ill.]
Aeration **2**: 316
Aerobic **1**: 108
Air pollution **1**: 2,
Algae **1**: 23, 143 [ill.]
Alignment **3**: 370
Alkaline **1**: 1
Amine **3**: 420
Ampere, Andre-Marie **2**: 185, 186 [ill.]
Amphibian **1**: 2, **2**: 342
Amplitude **4**: 589
Anaerobic **1**: 108
Andromeda Galaxy **2**: 278 [ill.]
Anemometer **4**: 746, 749 [ill.], 760 [ill.]
Animalcules **3**: 387
Annual growth **1**: 19-34
Anthocyanin **1**: 92
Antibodies **3**: 422
Aquifer **2**: 307, **4**: 729
Arch **4**: 634
Archimedes **1**: 125 [ill.]
Arrhenius, Svante **2**: 291
Artesian well **2**: 308

Artwork from Pompeii **4**: 686 [ill.]
Asexual reproduction **4**: 665
Astronomers **4**: 603
Astronomy **4**: 603
Atmosphere **2**: 291
Atmospheric pressure **4**: 745
Atoms **1**: 61, **2**: 203, **3**: 461, **4**: 615
Autotrophs **1**: 23
Auxins **4**: 648 [ill.], 666, 668 [ill.]

Bold type indicates volume number; [ill.] indicates illustration or photograph.

B

Bacteria **3**: 387
Barometer **4**: 762
Base **1**: 1, 76, **3**: 477
Batteries **3**: 462 [ill.]
Beam **4**: 635
Bean vine **4**: 649 [ill.]
Beriberi **3**: 420
Bernoulli, Daniel **2**: 250
Biochemical oxygen demand (BOD$_5$) **1**: 141
Biodegradable **1**: 108
Biomes **1**: 35-47
Bloodstream **3**: 446 [ill.]
Bond **1**: 61
Braided rivers **4**: 715
Bread dough **2**: 219 [ill.]
Bridge **4**: 636 [ill.]
Brine shrimp **1**: 4,

experiment
CENTRAL

lxxv

general index

Buoyancy **1:** 123-138, 124 [ill.], **3:** 545
Butterfly **2:** 342 [ill.]
By-products **2:** 300

C

Camera **4:** 607
Capillary action **4:** 699
Carbohydrates **3:** 421
Carbon dioxide **1:** 3
Carbon monoxide **1:** 3,
Carnivore **4:** 668
Carotene **1:** 92, **3:** 494
Catalysts **2:** 217
Caterpillar **2:** 341 [ill.]
Celestial bodies **1:** 175
Cells **1:** 49-59
Cell membrane **1:** 51
Centrifuge **3:** 404
Channel **4:** 715
Chanute, Octave **2:** 251
Cheese curd **3:** 390 [ill.]
Chemicals **1:** 1,
Chemical energy **1:** 61-74, **3:** 509
Chemical properties **1:** 75
Chemical reaction **1:** 61, 75, 77 [ill.]
Chlorophyll **1:** 91-104, 265, **3:** 493
Chloroplasts **1:** 52, 91, **3:** 493
Chromatography **1:** 93
Cleavage **3:** 533
Climate **4:** 745
Clouds **4:** 748 [ill.]
Coagulation **2:** 316, **3:** 405
Cohesion **4:** 697, 698 [ill.]
Colloid **3:** 403
Combustion **1:** 62, **2:** 300
Complete metamorphosis **2:** 341
Compost pile **1:** 106 [ill.], 107 [ill.]
Composting **1:** 105-121
Compression **4:** 635
Concave **3:** 433
Concentration **3:** 445
Condense/condensation **4:** 729
Conduction **2:** 323
Conductors **4:** 615
Confined aquifer **2:** 308, 310 [ill.]
Coniferous trees **1:** 36 [ill.]

Constellations **4:** 604
Continental drift **4:** 684
Control experiment **1:** 2, **3:** 560
Convection **2:** 325, 326 [ill.]
Convection current **2:** 326, **4:** 684
Convex **3:** 433
Corona **1:** 177
Cotyledon **2:** 265
Crust **3:** 528
Current **4:** 615
Cyanobacteria **1:** 23
Cycles **1:** 175
Cytology **1:** 50
Cytoplasm **1:** 51 [ill.], 51

D

Darwin, Charles **4:** 647, 647 [ill.], 667
Da Vinci, Leonardo **2:** 249 [ill.]
Decanting **3:** 404
Decibel(dB) **4:** 590
Decomposition **1:** 75, 108
Decomposition reaction **1:** 76
Density **1:** 123-138, 124 [ill.], **3:** 542, **4:** 746
Detergent between water and grease **4:** 700 [ill.]
Dependent variable **3:** 560
Desert **1:** 35
Dewpoint **4:** 729
Dicot **1:** 56 [ill.]
Diffraction **2:** 360
Diffraction grating **2:** 363
Diffusion **3:** 445-459
Disinfection **2:** 316
Dissolved oxygen (DO) **1:** 139-158
Distillation **3:** 404
DNA (deoxyribonucleic acid) **1:** 51 [ill.], 52
Domains **3:** 369, 370 [ill.]
Dormancy **1:** 20, **2:** 263
Drought **2:** 232
Drum **4:** 590 [ill.]
Dry cell **2:** 187
Dust Bowl **2:** 232
Dynamic equilibrium **3:** 447

experiment
CENTRAL

E

Ear, inside of human **4**: 592 [ill.]
Earthquakes **1**: 159-174, 160 [ill.],
   161 [ill.]
Eclipses **1**: 175-184
Ecologists **2**: 343
Ecosystem **1**: 143, **4**: 748
Electric charge repulsion **3**: 403
Electric eel **2**: 218
Electrical energy **3**: 509
Electricity **2**: 185-201, 302, **4**: 615
Electric motor **2**: 215 [ill.]
Electrode **2**: 186
Electrolyte **2**: 186
Electromagnetic spectrum **2**: 204 [ill.],
   205, 357, **3**: 431
Electromagnetic wavelength **2**: 204
   [ill.], **3**: 431
Electromagnet **2**: 214 [ill.],
   372 [ill.]
Electromagnetism **2**: 203-216, 326,
   3: 371
Electrons **2**: 185, 203, 461, **4**: 615
Electroscope **4**: 619, 620 [ill.]
Elevation **1**: 141
Ellips **2**: 278
Embryo **2**: 263
Endothermic reaction **1**: 61,
   63 [ill.], 79
Energy **3**: 509
Enzymes **2**: 217-230
Enzymology **2**: 219
Ephemerals **1**: 37
Epicenter **1**: 160
Equilibrium **4**: 634
Erosion **2**: 231-247
Escher, M.C. illusion **3**: 443 [ill.]
Euphotic zone **3**: 495
Eutrophication **1**: 141
Evaporate/evaporation **3**: 404,
   4: 737 [ill.]
Exothermic reaction **1**: 61, 62,
   63 [ill.], 79
Experiment **3**: 560

F

Fault **1**: 159
Fault blocks **1**: 159
Filtration **2**: 316, 404
Fireworks **1**: 78
Flammability **1**: 77
Flight **2**: 249-261
Fluorescence **2**: 360
Focal length **3**: 432, 434 [ill.]
Focal point **3**: 432
Food web **4**: 650
Force **2**: 278
Forest **1**: 35
Fossil fuels **1**: 1, 292
Fourier, Jean-Baptiste-Joseph **2**: 291
Fracture **3**: 533
Franklin, Benjamin **4**: 617 [ill.]
Frequency **2**: 204, **4**: 589
Friction **4**: 615
Frogs **2**: 343 [ill.]
Fronts **4**: 762
Fungus **1**: 23

G

Galaxy **4**: 605
Galilei, Galileo **4**: 603, 604 [ill.]
Genes **1**: 19
Genetic material **4**: 665
Geology **3**: 528
Geotropism **4**: 648
Germ theory of disease **3**: 388
Germination **2**: 263-276
Gibbous moon **1**: 182
Glacier **2**: 293
Global warming **2**: 292
Glucose **3**: 494
Golgi body **1**: 52
Grassland **1**: 35
Gravity **2**: 277-290
Greenhouse **2**: 292 [ill.], 667 [ill.]
Greenhouse effect **2**: 291-306, **4**: 576
Greenhouse gases **2**: 294
Groundwater **2**: 308 [ill.], 309 [ill.]
Groundwater aquifers **2**: 307-321
Growth rings (trees) **1**: 20

Bold type indicates volume number.

general index

H

Halley, Edmond **1**: 176
Heat **1**: 61, 323-339
Heat energy **2**: 323
Helium balloon **3**: 446 [ill.]
Herbivore **4**: 668
Hertz (Hz) **4**: 589
Heterotrophs **1**: 23
High air pressure **4**: 762
H.M.S. Challenger **3**: 542 [ill.]
Hooke, Robert **1**: 49
Hormone **4**: 648, 666
Hot air balloon **2**: 325 [ill.]
Humidity **4**: 745
Humus **1**: 105, 107
Hutton, James **3**: 527, 528 [ill.]
Hydrogen peroxide **2**: 221 [ill.]
Hydrologic cycle **4**: 713, 729
Hydrologists **4**: 730
Hydrology **4**: 729
Hydrometer **3**: 543
Hydrophilic **4**: 699
Hydrophobic **4**: 699
Hydrotropism **4**: 649
Hypertonic solution **3**: 447
Hypotonic solution **3**: 447

I

Igneous rock **3**: 528
Immiscible **1**: 125
Impermeable **2**: 307
Impurities **2**: 316
Incomplete metamorphosis **2**: 341
Independent variable **3**: 560
Indicator **3**: 479
Inertia **2**: 278
Infrared radiation **2**: 291, 326
Ingenhousz, Jan **3**: 493, 494 [ill.]
Inner core **3**: 528
Inorganic **2**: 233
Insulation/insulator **2**: 185, 291, **4**: 615
Interference fringes **2**: 359
Ions **1**: 1, 185, 403, 477
Ionic conduction **2**: 185
Isobars **4**: 762
Isotonic solutions **3**: 447

J

Janssen, Hans **1**: 49

K

Kinetic energy **3**: 509-525
Kuhne, Willy **2**: 217

L

Landfills **1**: 105-121, 108 [ill.]
Langley, Samuel Pierpont **2**: 251
Larva **2**: 341
Lava **3**: 528, 529 [ill.], 683
Leaves **1**: 92, 93 [ill.]
Leeuwenhoek, Anton van **1**: 49, 387
Lens **1**: 49, 50 [ill.]
Lichens **1**: 22 [ill.], 22
Life cycles **2**: 341-356
Lift **2**: 250
Light **2**: 357
Lightening **4**: 618 [ill.]
Light-year **4**: 604
Lilienthal, Otto **2**: 250 [ill.]
Lind, James **3**: 420 [ill.]
Lippershey, Hans **1**: 49
Litmus paper **3**: 479
Local Group, The **4**: 606
Lockyer, Joseph Norman **1**: 178 [ill.]
Low air pressure **4**: 762
Luminescence **1**: 79
Lunar eclipse **1**: 177 [ill.]
    partial lunar eclipse **1**: 178
    total lunar eclipse **1**: 177
Luster **3**: 533

M

Macroorganisms **1**: 106
Magma **3**: 528, 684
Magma chambers **4**: 684
Magma surge **4**: 686
Magnet **3**: 370 [ill.]
Magnetic circuit **3**: 371
Magnetic field **2**: 203, **3**: 369
Magnetic resonance imaging (MRI) **2**: 205 [ill.]
Magnetism **3**: 369-385
Mantle **3**: 528

Manure 1: 105
Maruia River 4: 715 [ill.]
Mass 1: 123, 278
Matter 1: 123, 4: 615
Meandering river 4: 715
Meniscus 4: 699
Metamorphic rock 3: 531
Metamorphosis 2: 341
Meteorologists 4: 747, 759
Meteorology 4: 762
Michell, John 1: 160
Microclimate 2: 294
Micromes 1: 106
Microorganisms 1: 105, 107, 108,
    3: 387-401, 389 [ill.]
Micropyle 2: 264
Microscopes 1: 49, 50 [ill.]
Milky Way 4: 603
Mineral 3: 527-539
Mixtures 3: 403-417, 404 [ill.]
Moh's hardness scale 3: 534
Molecules 1: 61, 3: 445
Molting 2: 341
Monocot 1: 56 [ill.]
Monument Valley 1: 37 [ill.]
Moon 1: 175
Mountain 3: 530 [ill.]
Mount Tolbachik (volcano)
    4: 685 [ill.]

N

Nanometer 3: 431
Nansen bottles 3: 544
Nebula 4: 604, 605 [ill.]
Neutralization 1: 3, 3: 477
Neutrons 3: 461
Newton, Isaac 2: 277 [ill.], 277, 357
    [ill.], 357, 3: 511
Niagrara Falls 4: 716 [ill.]
Nile river 4: 714 [ill.]
Nonpoint source 2: 310
Nucleus 1: 51, 4: 615
Nutrient 3: 419
Nutrition 3: 419-429
Nymphs 2: 341

O

Oceanography 3: 541
Oersted, Hans Christian 3: 370 [ill.]
Optical illusions 3: 431-444, 440 [ill.],
    443 [ill.]
Optics 3: 431-444
Organelles 1: 52
Organic 2: 233
Organic waste 1: 105
Orion Nebula 4: 605 [ill.]
Osmosis 3: 445-459
Outer core 3: 528
Oxidation 3: 461
Oxidation-reduction 3: 461-476
Oxidation state 3: 461
Oxidizing agent 3: 463
Ozone layer 2: 291-306, 4: 576

P

Passive solar energy system 4: 576
Pasteurization 3: 388
Pasteur, Louis 3: 388 [ill.]
Peaks 2: 204
Penicillin 3: 389
Pepsin 2: 218
Percolate 2: 307
Permeable 2: 307
PH 1: 1, 477-491
Pharmacology 1: 91
Phases 1: 182 [ill.]
Phloem 3: 494
PH levels in U.S. 1: 5 [ill.]
PH meter 3: 479 [ill.]
Phosphorescence 2: 360
Photography 3: 433 [ill.]
Photosynthesis 1: 23, 91, 139, 3: 493-
    507, 494 [ill.], 4: 649
Phototropism 4: 647
Photovoltaic cells 4: 577
Physical change 1: 75, 76 [ill.]
Physical properties 1: 75
Physiologists 3: 493
Phytoplankton 1: 139, 3: 495 [ill.], 495
Pigment 3: 493

general index

Bold type indicates volume number.

general index

general index

Bold type indicates volume number.